D0997073

A MUSICIAN'S ALPHABET

A Musician's Alphabet

SUSAN TOMES

faber and faber

First published in 2006
by Faber and Faber Limited
3 Queen Square London WC1N 3AU

Typeset by Faber and Faber Limited
Printed in England by Mackays of Chatham, plc

A CIP record for this book
is available from the British Library

ISBN 978-0-571-22883-6
ISBN 0-571-22883-6

2 4 6 8 10 9 7 5 3 1

For Bob and for Maya

A is for Audience

Whenever I go to a classical concert as part of the audience, and find myself planning what clothes to wear, I realise that I am subject to mysterious rules. Why should it matter what I wear when I'm only going to listen?

When I am actually playing in the concert, clothes seem even more crucial. One of my recurrent dreams is that my luggage goes astray on the way to the concert and that I have to walk on stage in my ordinary clothes. No silk, no high heels, no jewellery or cosmetics. I did once turn up for a music festival having left my whole array of concert clothes folded neatly on the bed at home. The festival was in a rural setting with no shops nearby. But I was staying with kind people who asked around, delved into their own wardrobes and put together several outfits I could borrow for the concerts. They were even more uncomfortable than I was about the prospect of me appearing on stage in jeans and a jumper.

What is actually going on when we worry about what clothes to wear for a concert? Clearly going to classical concerts has a social meaning as well as a musical one. I like to think I'm ignoring the former in favour of the latter. But I still seem to have a finely calibrated sense of how formal I may (or must) look, both when I'm in the audience and when I'm on the stage. As a listener I must look smart, but not as smart as the performers. When I am a performer, I must look more special than the listeners. These cultural modes vary from country to country. In some Mediterranean cities, the audience dresses up extravagantly to attend a concert. Sometimes they are so lacquered, so bouffant, so dripping with gold and fragrant with expensive perfume that we performers in our much-used concert clothes feel positively underdressed. No matter how well you play, and how focused you are on the music, it is not a good feeling if the audience looks as if they consider the occasion more important than you do.

That we all consider the occasion important is demonstrated in many different ways. The musicians show it in their dignified demeanour on stage, their deportment as they walk on and off, their tactful blend of modesty, grandeur and friendliness. The audience show it in their silence and good behaviour. For the last century it has been the done thing to listen to a classical performance in rapt silence. It wasn't always so, but it is so now. The music is felt to be a precious cultural possession, and the audience acknowledges the importance of the performance by being still. At other kinds of concerts, with other kinds of music, it is different. The audience's participation is welcomed. But in classical concerts it is felt to be disturbing and wrong if anyone makes a noise or moves around; both the musicians and the rest of the audience will protest if this happens.

When I was little I sometimes played my piano pieces to friends of my parents who came round for coffee. My performance was surrounded by chat, and I didn't dress up. But as soon as public performance came into the question, the subject of special clothes and behaviour arose. It was somehow linked with tickets, money, the fact that people had actually paid to come and listen in a special building. The same people who might have eaten biscuits in our living room as they listened to my piano piece would have to go to a box office, buy a ticket, put on smart clothes and sit in silence to hear me doing the same thing in a concert hall. Clearly they were buying into more than an opportunity to hear music played.

I still think of this phenomenon today when concert promoters offer artists a complimentary ticket for a member of their family. It's understood that a player's family cannot be expected to pay full price every time they come to give moral support. Yet they get the same experience, the same comfortable seat in the concert hall, as the people who've paid money, and indeed, their being there may prevent someone from buying a ticket. Sometimes, if I have a guest ticket but no guests, I give it to someone in the ticket queue. They're always happy, of course. But the random nature of the gift no longer pleases me. I fret about whether some other person in the queue deserved it more. The whole ticket-buying transaction starts to bother me. I'm aware that if I got my hands on dozens of guest tickets and gave them all away to strangers, there would come a point when the management would inform me that there was no income out of which I could be paid for playing the concert. And this would distress me more than giving away lots of free tickets would please me. Meanwhile, I feel that as long as people are parting with hard-earned cash to hear me, the least I can do is go out and buy some colourful silk thing to wear. And don't get me started on the expectations placed on women! Why do I feel I need to vary my outfit from concert to concert, when my male colleagues wear the same suits night after night for years on end? Nobody insists that I vary my outfits, but from the comments people make, and from the way that they seem to keep track of what I wore on this or that occasion, I feel the imperative as clearly as if it were written into the contract.

The fact that we seem to need a special building in which to listen to music (or to look at paintings, or to watch people dance) is a whole sociological and economic subject of its own. I still remember my surprise on encountering my first 'real' concert hall. Until then, any performances had taken place in rooms where the listeners and I entered by the same door and were literally on the same level. The concert hall, however, had its own apartheid. There were two entrances, one for the audience (at the front) and another for the players (at the back). This didn't seem fitting. Artists at the back? Once inside the building, I realised that the artists' entrances were at the back because they gave on to the dressing rooms and rehearsal spaces behind the stage. Here one was isolated from the public, who had their own foyer at the front of the building. As a player one need never, in fact, meet the audience face to face! This was supposed to be a protection, but it came as a disappointment. One arrived on stage through a special door, usually to find oneself elevated above the audience. Going through this door (just after the house lights were dimmed) became a moment of enormous, nerve-racking importance. Judy Garland in one of her late films shows us the way she had to stand in the wings and summon up the nervous charge she needed to burst on to the stage. Seeing her revving up like a motorbike made me smile at the memory of all the doors behind which I and my colleagues had stood, jiggling from foot to foot, checking that we had everything, trying to calm nervous stomachs.

Are we there for the audience, or are they there for us? The music can be played without them, and usually is – in private practice and rehearsal. But this is neither a performance nor an event. A performance cannot take place without an audience, and to make the performance feel like an event depends on the willing collaboration of the listeners. Moreover, an audience is needed to generate money for the musicians. The days of court or aristocratic patronage are gone, and musicians need to get money from somewhere. The fact that we depend on audiences for our living should make us bend over backwards to please them, but it is not nearly so simple. We want them to please us too. I even have a musician friend who claims to despise the audience for admiring him, but that's another story – his, not theirs.

These days, because so much music is available on disc, people do not actually need to come to the concert hall to hear music. But they like to come for all sorts of reasons, ranging from the social to the artistic. If you watch the New Year's Day concert from Vienna on television, you will be struck by the look and demeanour of the audience. Expensively dressed, indistinguishable from one another, perfectly behaved with no unseemly displays of emotion or surprise, they run every year through a well-drilled repertoire of responses to the familiar sequence of music by the Strauss family. These days one can see all kinds of nationalities in the audience, but they dress and behave exactly like the Viennese. People go to enormous lengths to get their hands on tickets. Members of the orchestra fight to be 'on' this particular date, because of the extra money paid for television rights around the world. The orchestra is, in fact, superb and the conductor is usually very fine too. But the meaning of the occasion is far beyond the programme of waltzes and polkas. It says, 'We can afford all this, and we know how to behave too. We are here to affirm the stability of this society.' People watching TV around the world are impressed that so many obviously powerful and wealthy people should have the time (and inclination) to sit perfectly still and listen in silence to music designed for dancing. The message is, 'Now we don't even need to dance. We have passed beyond frivolity to a place where our status is its own spectacle.'

This is an extreme example, of course. Every concert hall (especially the symphony hall and the opera house) contains its quota of people who are there to see and be seen, and if one is honest, there is probably an element of this for everyone present, including the performers. But there are also many listeners who ignore the social benefits and hungrily concentrate on the performance alone. For them, wearing nice clothes is just an annoying convention at an otherwise cherished event. In many cases, they know the music already. But no matter how many times they have heard it on disc, or studied the musical score, these things are not substitutes for a performance. So concert-goers look forward to the moment when the sound will be created in the same room as them. The sound waves produced by the musicians playing their instruments will pass through the air and touch their bodies. They will see and hear the musicians interact in a unique, never-to-be-repeated way. And though listeners don't participate in the performance, their close attention certainly contributes to, indeed largely brings about, a shared concentration which enables transcendental things to happen. This can never be the case with records, no matter how much one loves the music. Concert-goers know all this and relish being physically present as music comes alive.

Musicians know it too and have a love-hate relationship with the audience because of it. Will tonight's audience help to create the conditions for a magical experience? Or will they cough, fidget, resent the social pressure that brought them here? Some musicians have to shut the audience out of their thoughts in order to play their best. Others have to let the audience in. If I find myself lacking in adrenalin, I sometimes sit in the dressing room between rehearsal and concert and make myself think about our listeners hurrying to finish up work, ironing clothes, instructing babysitters, preparing early or late suppers, making arrangements for transport and parking, how to meet friends. Imagining all this makes me realise how much care the audience puts into a concert. They think they are coming to spend an evening listening to me, but equally, I am preparing to spend an evening in their company.

B is for Background Music

Background music is a kind of epidemic of our time. For some reason, those who run public buildings and spaces seem to feel that they must perfume – or should that be poison? – the air with unsolicited music to keep us docile. A whole species of 'muzak' is now specially composed to be narcotically bland, deliberately not quite interesting enough to distract us from buying things.

For many people, one of the chief irritations about background music is that they don't choose it. They don't choose to hear it, and they don't choose what is played. Musicians are often especially sensitive to background music, but there's an additional kind they have to suffer. No external sound source is needed, because it plays inside rather than outside their heads.

Over the years, many people have asked me what piece of music it is that I'm playing on the table top with my fingers, or humming under my breath. Sometimes they've been surprised, perhaps offended, that I could be thinking of a piece of music while I'm supposed to be taking part in a conversation. And yet often when they ask me, I'm not even aware that I am following a piece in my head while also listening to them. It's become an automatic process, like that of digestion – essential but unconscious.

Playing on the dining table is only the tip of the iceberg.

Like most musicians, I have music playing in my head most of the time whether I like it or not. It's a kind of multitasking that comes naturally. To some extent it's how I practise things, or how I digest them. Many's the time I've gone back to the piano to find that a tricky piece of fingering has sweetly embedded itself in my memory. But it isn't always so focused; there's a whole library of works that randomly get selected and played. They can be just fragments or sometimes whole movements. And, of course, I am only a performer, my mental library more or less restricted to works that already exist, and to random melodies that are clearly bits and pieces of folk songs reassembled. No doubt a composer could say a lot more about how original music arises in the head.

I once visited a friend who works as a clairvoyant. She offered to do a sketch of the 'astral colours' she saw around my body. As she was drawing with her box of pastel-coloured chalks, I asked her whether she always sees these colours around people. 'Yes,' she replied. 'Doesn't it distract you terribly?' I wanted to know. 'Well, let me ask you this,' she said. 'Do you have music playing in your head all the time?' 'Yes,' I said. 'Does it distract you terribly?' she asked. 'No,' I said. 'It's just the same with me,' she said. 'I see the colours, but I can tune them out if I want to participate in ordinary life. It must be the same for you with music.' And so it is.

It's strange that one can speak of 'music playing' in one's head when actually there is no sound there at all. I say that I hear it, but not in the usual sense of using my ears; I just imagine it. I suppose all artists are like this. Painters must 'see' paintings that don't exist yet, and writers must 'see' passages of text. Yet in the cases of prose and painting, both the imagined work of art and the actual one are silent, even though prose clearly relates to speech, and can be read aloud. It does not seem contradictory to speak of 'seeing' a drawing or a page of prose. But to speak of silently 'hearing' a piece of music is more paradoxical, because sound is what defines music – isn't it? There's a big difference between an imaginary piece of music and one that actually sounds in the outside world. To read a music score in your head is not a replacement for hearing it played. Can we really speak of listening to music if there is no sound? If music is silent and is only imagined, does it lose its essential nature and become something else, like architecture or philosophy?

I've noticed that when I recall a piece of orchestral music, I have a haphazard sense of its original instrumental colours. As a student I always had difficulty with orchestral scoring, finding it hard to imagine which combinations of tone colours from which instruments would be exactly right. Now, when I play a symphony in my head, I hear it with the orchestral scoring subtracted. The pitches and harmonies are there, but not the superimposed sound of oboes, strings or brass. Even the fact that I use the word 'superimposed' shows that the instrumental timbres are not, for me, intrinsic to the musical thought. Though the instrumental colours of an orchestral work are vivid to me when I first hear it, my musical memory subsequently transforms them into piano music, though with the piano sound subtracted.

This is real hair-splitting stuff: I seem to be speaking of the difference between orchestral music with the tone colours subtracted, and piano music with the tone colour subtracted. Isn't that a bit like claiming that I can tell the difference between a fork that isn't there, and a knife which isn't there? I can only say that it's a matter of transforming that musical material in my imagination into something that I can feel in my fingers; in other words, towards the medium of piano music, which I understand better. The particularity of which instrument plays what in an orchestral piece doesn't appear to be central to my enjoyment. I respond to other things, such as mood, emotion, narrative sense, form, timing, expression, phrasing, and associations.

Recently I started to think about the way my subconscious selects things to play from my large but fragmented mental library. One of the simplest triggers is the pace of what I'm doing. Without consciously noticing that there is a rhythm to my movement – swimming, cooking, gardening – the music that plays in my head matches it, as though it were a perfectly coordinated soundtrack. That's background music at its most basic. It can work the other way round, too, making me speed up the motion of chopping or washing in order to fit the rhythm of the music playing in my head. At a more sophisticated level, there are fragments of music unconsciously chosen to sum up the end of a conversation, to express a mood, or to be a metaphor.

Many of my musician friends report that their interior lives are accompanied by illustrative background music. Recently a friend of mine had to attend an inquest after the death of a close relative. She reported afterwards that during the inquest she kept 'hearing' the Prelude from one of the Bach Suites for solo cello. She had always thought of this particular Prelude as being in itself a kind of musical journey, and it arose at that moment as a metaphor for the shape and journey of someone's life. Undoubtedly this musical narrative helped her through a difficult event, and it was therapeutic for her to feel that a person's life can have a musical shape.

In my case, the American musical has proved a treasury of references. Daily activities often tap into song lyrics I didn't know I had memorised, and I find myself singing something appropriate, like Rodgers and Hart's 'There's a Small Hotel' when I'm booking accommodation. More interestingly, I also hear appropriate songs in the background as coded messages to let me know what I'm really feeling. 'Stormy Weather', for example, has more than once turned itself on as a warning. 'You'd Be So Nice To Come Home To' and 'Someone To Watch Over Me' have alerted me to positive feelings. But once called up, these fragments of music often refuse to leave. A key word may summon some apposite music, but that music then gets stuck in the foreground of my musical memory, playing over and over again. Often just a crucial chord sequence, or a twist in the melody – in other words a fragment of the fragment – repeats so often that it becomes hypnotic. With me a tapestry of those fragments, sometimes repeated for hours, forms a kind of fabric on which other thoughts are snagged.

Some years ago I was preparing to make a recording of syncopated 1930s piano music by Billy Mayerl. His catchy tunes and rhythms proved all too catchy while I was in the throes of polishing them up. They played over and over in my head so unstoppably that they interfered with my ability to sleep. It was ghastly lying awake in the small hours, tormented by jolly music. Finally my doctor sent me to a specialist in self-hypnosis, who taught me some relaxation techniques. It was only after I became fairly adept at these techniques that the once benign, now frighteningly jolly tunes began to depart from my inner ear. This was a process that had clearly gone beyond 'practising' or 'digesting', and that experience shows how deeply we can get bound up with the material we play.

I've become more aware recently of music that arises as a barrier between me and the rest of the world. Again, this is not something I can consciously order, but it seems to come to my rescue in certain situations. These can be as harmless as shopping: I can go round the supermarket looking as if I'm choosing groceries, when what I'm *really* doing is listening to a piece of Schumann, with groceries as a superficial counterpoint. In this case music seems to work to keep boredom at bay. At other times, difficult times, it seems to insulate me from a tense situation like a meeting I'm worried about, or an argument. It doesn't stop me from thinking and speaking, and looking fairly normal on the outside, but it seems to cushion me from excessive anxiety. In these situations it doesn't seem important what music is playing, just that *something* is – but it must be something coherent. It has to be music whose sense of flow carries me onwards through a sticky situation. The jarring randomness and unpredictability of external events is soothed by an internal narrative of music. Music flows through awkward gaps and pauses in the real world, comforting me with the sense that there is another way to pass through these moments.

Now commercially produced background music is everywhere – on every station, in every shopping mall, in restaurants, cinemas, airports and leisure centres. It proposes a feelgood state based on anaesthesia. Many people dislike it because it has no relevance to their mood. At least my background music has profound links to what's going on in my life. I may not choose it, but I know that it's a powerful commentary.

C is for Chamber Music

How to write about chamber music, the family of pieces that won my heart when I was a youngster, and which has been at the centre of my performing life? These days, when anyone alludes to the fact that chamber music is 'difficult' or 'elitist', I often recall that first effortless sense of liking. Our educational work as musicians tries to address the question of why young people don't naturally gravitate towards chamber music, and need to be gently and persuasively introduced to it. I'm ill-equipped for this kind of outreach work because I don't remember ever having had doubts about chamber music. Nobody had to use their imagination to convert me. I saw the point straight away, and took it for granted that everyone else did too.

'The point' was really that many composers used chamber music to give us the truest portraits of themselves, their most intimate thoughts and feelings. There was no sense of showing off such as might occur in solo repertoire; nor was there the multiplication of means and effects which sometimes makes orchestral music seem coarse. Instead, there was a wonderful conversation between people with meaningful things to say. With one person on each part, everyone was vital, and each player influenced the others in an unpredictable way. Playing chamber music was like digesting life in the company of a newly acquired family. At junior music college and on music courses, I always particularly looked forward to my chamber music sessions, which gradually overtook everything else in importance.

But we in the Florestan Trio (violin, cello and piano) did agree recently that the term 'chamber music' has somehow acquired an unhelpful tinge over the years. We've noticed that when we describe ourselves as a chamber group, there's a slight blankness in people's response. The word 'chamber', once used to denote music that was played at home or in a smaller room, is no longer part of everyday vocabulary. Chamber group? Somehow the terminology has gone a bit stale. Yet it doesn't help very much to say instead that we play 'in a trio'. A trio? The question often hangs in the air. A trio of what? If I say, 'a piano trio', people sometimes ask whether I mean three pianos. Yes, the names are a bit of a handicap, but it would seem artificial to start calling ourselves by a name as cool and urban as a pop group's. Though we love the music as much as ever, we identify less and less with the terms 'chamber group', 'chamber musicians', and 'chamber music'. Percy Grainger's alternative of 'room music' doesn't make our hearts leap either.

Now, I have an axe to grind about chamber groups and their difficulties in reaching large audiences. Everyone tells us that our kind of music is less popular than symphonies and operas because it uses small forces and lacks impact. We are supposed to be philosophical about this and content ourselves with small audiences. However, if you look at the world of popular music you find that small groups are by far the dominant force, rulers of the airwaves and darlings of the media. From The Beatles and The Rolling Stones through The Beach Boys and ABBA to U2 and Coldplay – it's exactly these groups of a few individuals that audiences love most. No single pop artist had the effect that The Beatles did together. The group formula is, in fact, so well recognised that cynical promoters can manufacture instant success by plucking the ingredients out of TV talent shows, putting together several attractive people and giving them a record contract. Even if they are mismatched, and even if they can't sing or play particularly well, the magic of 'the group' will guarantee success. DJs predict that their first single will go to No. 1 in the pop charts before they've even recorded it. They will become celebrities, their photos everywhere just because they are that alluring thing, a new group. I know teenagers who refer to someone in tones of reverence just because they are 'in a group'. Even a despised contemporary will acquire social cachet if they become a group member.

I find groups just as interesting as everyone else does. Groups are alternative families, with their different characters, their rows, their intimacy, their loyalty. We find the dynamic endlessly fascinating. The same principle works in all the successful TV sitcoms. *Friends*, *Seinfeld*, *Frasier*, *ER*, *Will and Grace*, *The Simpsons*, *The Sopranos* and all the British soaps are based on the tug-of-war/tug-of-love scenario that seems to go along with being a family. Watching accomplished actors in these sitcoms is for me very much like watching a skilful group of chamber musicians at work. There's something musical about the rhythm and pace of their interactions. They listen, they react, they wait, they surge forward, they bounce off one another's ideas. They each represent some different facet of human nature. They have to know when to be centre-stage, when to support, when to be in the background. There are only a few of them, and the audience doesn't want anyone to be added or subtracted; they tend to resent actors brought in to be someone's new partner or whatever. The integrity of the original group is really important to fans.

In other words, the 'chamber group' in the worlds of pop music and TV drama is actually the king. Actors and musicians are desperate to get into those groups because they know how powerful they will become as a part of it. The whole will become more than the sum of its parts. So why, in the world of classical music, are chamber groups not similarly idolised? We can play our instruments, we have years of experience, we spend time getting the mixture of players right, we're devoted to our art, and we have fantastic music to play. To continue the 'family' analogy, we could say that a chamber group is like a family whose members always say, in music, different and interesting things. (Compared with this, a pop group is like a family that always agrees with one another.) It could even be that our private lives are quite interesting too. Yet in the world of classical music, a small group is a small group is a small group. It's smaller and quieter than an orchestra, yet at the same time, not three or four times as interesting as a solo artist. A chamber ensemble is perceived as voluntarily having exiled itself into remote territory. It will never make the headlines because each member has just signed a contract to do the next series for five million dollars per episode.

Perhaps it is as simple as this: pop music is loud, amplified, and has voices. TV sitcoms are generally loud, amplified, and have voices. By contrast, chamber music is quiet, unamplified, and has no voices. The lack of voices should not be confused with the lack of something to say, of course. I never noticed the absence of voices in chamber music because I always felt there was a message in the music, and to hear it delivered by instruments was a delightful bonus.

Perhaps it is a sociological thing. In the past, before recordings were invented, people only heard music if it was played by someone in their presence. Music-making was largely domestic. In the countries that gave birth to the repertoire I play, many people learned to play instruments and enjoyed getting together with family members and friends to play music. There was, indeed, no other way of hearing music except on the rare occasions when visiting artists came to your town. If you attended a concert, it would be a sophisticated version of something you were familiar with from amateur music-making at home.

Today, however, most people's experience of music is beyond what is achievable domestically. Most people now hear the bulk of their music on CD, radio, personal stereo. Not only is it amplified, but because recording artists are aware that they must meet international standards of performance, it's played to a high technical level. It is also edited and manipulated in the studio to produce something impossibly perfect and glossy. Nobody can reproduce this at home through their own efforts. Amateur music-making is no longer the prevailing standard as it once was, and this is a big change. Professional music-making used to be a more accomplished version of something you had tried yourself, but now it has become a highly sophisticated version of something *of which most people have no experience*.

Lots of people today enjoy having a go at playing pop or rock music. It's an important hobby, which they're proud of. They play in pubs, clubs, garages and teenage bedrooms.

A professional pop group is a slicker version of what they do, better managed and presented, but recognisably engaged in the same activity. But we chamber musicians, playing music from one or two centuries ago, sometimes sense the gulf that has opened up between players and listeners. Certainly there are still people who play chamber music with friends and family, but it is not nearly so common as it used to be. Thanks to recordings, we all know how the best players play, and many people have discreetly abandoned the field to the professionals, feeling that if they want to listen to this type of music, there are lots of great performances on disc, much better than anything they could achieve themselves at home.

The more people lose their collective memory of amateur music-making, the more they feel respectfully alienated from professionals such as us. The knowledge that these masterpieces are shared by all music-lovers is gradually being replaced by a feeling that they belong to the experts. This is sad, because it was amateur music-making that turned most professionals on to chamber music in the first place. I, for example, never went to a concert of chamber music by professionals until I had been enjoying chamber music for quite a while as a participant. When I did go to a concert I didn't see the players as remote, nor was I intimidated by them, because I had already discovered that I and my friends could do a pretty good job of playing that music ourselves. But because of changes in music education, fewer people are now in that position. Today I sometimes see the audience looking at us as if they are thinking the famous words that are sung in Schoenberg's second string quartet: 'I feel air from another planet.'

D is for Difficulty

I have been asked to play a Mozart piano concerto, K488 in A major, which I first learned and performed when I was ten or eleven years old, but have hardly looked at for many years. It's one of those pieces which, painstakingly learned at an early age, became one of the foundation stones of my repertoire. When I first learned it, it must have been one of the most difficult things I had tackled. Now, with so many other musical challenges faced in the intervening years, you would think it would be easy to come back to the Mozart. But annoyingly, it isn't easy at all.

I still have the very copy I used when I was a child, the pages now so fragile they have melted away from their bindings. It's an edition favoured by my first piano teacher, who thought it was a trusty piece of scholarship, but which now seems encrusted with unnecessary additions. Mind you, I only know that they are additions when I compare the old edition with a more recent one. The naughty editors have not made clear what is original and what has been added or changed. Indeed, they say in the preface that their chief task has been to 'modernise' the score, 'improving the fingering' and 'amplifying the expression marks' to bring them up to date. This was done in the 1920s, decades before the period-instrument movement made us aware of our cultural, or perhaps temporal, arrogance: 'We live at a later time, so we know better.' For example, the editors of my old edition have actually changed the tempo markings at the start of each movement, clearly finding Mozart's simple indications too elementary. His 'Andante' has been expanded into 'Andante semplice ma molto espressivo', and 'Allegro assai' has become 'Presto grazioso e brillante'. Talk about putting words into the composer's mouth!

As I practise this piece, time seems to fold in on itself and I am launched back to the feeling of practising it long ago. Well, not the feeling so much as the physical sensation. And in particular, there are fast passages where I stumble as though there is a built-in difficulty. Very annoyingly, my old edition contains pencilled remarks from my childhood piano teacher drawing my attention to these very bits. 'This!!' she has written above certain passages, meaning, 'I keep telling you to practise this and it is still not right!' Or, 'for next week!' I can hardly believe that not only the next week, but forty years later I still stumble at those very same bits. Has my technique really not improved in the intervening years?

When I ponder this, I realise that by contrast there are in fact plenty of pieces that were once difficult for me, but which I have managed to master. I recall, for instance, a long period when two college friends and I were learning Ravel's piano trio. I thought that there were certain passages in the piano part I would never be able to play at the required speed. Nevertheless, by analysing the physical movements needed, by gradually increasing the tempo, by digesting the musical content and being able to step back mentally, I did discover how to do it. The knowledge became built in to my experience of the piece, and I now understand how to surmount its technical challenges. This seems to show that I have learned something over the years. With the Schubert E flat trio, with Schumann's big solo piano works such as *Kreisleriana* or the *Humoreske*, with Beethoven's 'Archduke' Trio, similar wrestling has taken place with more or less satisfying results. I have learned how to pace myself so that stamina is no longer a problem in performance. I have been able to grade the amount of muscle power needed at given moments, so that I am not using too little or too much at inappropriate times. This is, I feel, a proper use of technical study – it should help you to be able to play as you want at the moment that you need to.

There seem to be pieces that get technically easier over time, and pieces that remain obstinately or inherently difficult. What is the nature of their difficulty, and why is it harder to overcome? I am not speaking here of musical or interpretative difficulty, which bears very little relation to whether something is technically difficult or not. Quite often, when rehearsing something technically hard, my chamber-music colleagues say to one another, 'Well, at least it isn't musically difficult.' Music which is technically but not musically difficult presents a solvable kind of challenge. Music which is difficult to interpret remains challenging long after the notes have been successfully learned. Pieces that are both technically and musically difficult often turn out, in fact, to be our long-term favourites – so deep is the bond formed by burrowing through their multiple layers.

In some music – in Mozart piano concertos, for example – there are passages where the hand stumbles, even after patient rehearsal. When I listen to other pianists playing these passages I often hear them falter in the same places.

It's not a matter of their being badly written for the piano, because they aren't. Indeed, the composer himself was a virtuoso performer, who would have played all these works and adjusted anything which he found awkward. His piano concertos are amongst my very favourite pieces of music. So perhaps I am simply more sensitive to my success with them than I am to other pieces, because they mean more to me? Whatever the reason, there seems to be something challenging about Mozart which demands constant alertness, even years after learning the music. Performing his works, one feels both very happy and very exposed. There is nowhere to hide, because he is one of those rare composers who writes no more than he means to say. There is no gratuitous dazzling such as one finds in lots of solo piano music.

The limpidity of Mozart's piano writing, which makes some people assume it is 'easy', is its biggest challenge. Compared with a barnstorming piece of Romantic piano music, there are relatively few notes on the page. Yet everything has to drop into place at exactly the right moment and with the right touch. There is not, as there may be with some Romantic composers, the opportunity to put down the pedal, fly around the figuration and create an impressive 'whoosh' of sound. Nor can you emphasise fast-changing harmonies or exploit rubato to distract attention from bumpiness in your playing of the melodic figurations. The personal spontaneity that characterises many Romantic piano works is all too easily overlaid with the pianist's own. A composer's whimsical outbursts may seem to justify an answering capriciousness in the player. In many works of the Classical era, however, and particularly in Mozart where beauty and proportion co-exist, self-expression is not paramount. Everything is so balanced and finely judged that if the pianist's hands behave waywardly, the mismatch between expression and content is glaringly obvious.

One difficulty in Mozart lies in the evenness of his fast passages, running semiquavers whose regular surface makes any asymmetry of touch instantly apparent. In his piano writing, he often makes the hand suddenly change direction after establishing a pattern of movement. Scale passages, for example, or repeated broken chord figuration, lull the hand into a sense of security. If Mozart then suddenly interrupts the pattern, demands that the hand should hop back and forth from white to black keys, or left and right, or play a trill, something has to be decoupled in the brain to make it possible. If there is time to think and plan, it's not too difficult, but if it happens at speed it requires a lightning ability to break the pattern – difficult for most of us at the best of times. These are often the places where pianists stumble, where a little eddy is inserted into a longer flow. As a pianist facing such a passage you have to remind yourself that there's a moment where you must not be complacent about your fluency. Sleight of hand is needed.

If you have trouble with such passages year after year, you are driven to look at them in microscopic detail. After long contemplation I have come to the conclusion that there is only one way to master them. You have to be poised ready above every note at the moment that you need to play it. Your hand has not to be in the middle of doing something else or preparing to go somewhere else. This means no muscle tension, derived from a previous movement or anticipating a future one, which may pull your hand or finger away from the next note. You have not to be *expecting* something else, but to accept and be in place for the note which actually comes next. This, however, does not mean that one is to approach any note with a passive attitude. Exponents of certain physical relaxation techniques sometimes play like this. Desperate not to import tension into their playing, they concentrate on physical comfort and thereby sometimes become inexpressive. That's not what I advocate at all. Rather, a good performer should know just what the music means at any given moment, how it relates to the whole shape, and how to supply just what it needs. The point is not so much physical comfort but rather balance and readiness.

Such awareness could, perhaps, be achieved if you have lots of time to contemplate each movement, as in a yoga or t'ai chi exercise. But in fact you have to manage everything at speed, in real time, as you keep pace with the music and with others playing it. If you look at it under a very searching light, you see that in both a physical and in a mental sense, you must shake off the demands of both the past and the future, so that there is nothing to do but be ready for the next note, at the place in the keyboard where it is. Lightning reflexes help, but the real art, as in a Zen meditation, lies in learning to be poised in each micro-second. To be ready for the next step as it occurs, not hoping for anything else, may seem a simple process. But before one can do it, it seems that one has to learn a lot of things and forget a lot of other things, preferably both at the same time.

E is for Entertainment

I was standing in the wings recently before a solo piano recital, running through passages of Schubert in my head, and listening to the chairman of the concert society telling the audience about the concert. He concluded by saying, 'We can look forward to a lovely evening's entertainment.' Entertainment! I felt myself bristling. That wasn't what I thought I was there to provide, but why not? I was there to play lovely music, but to be honest I don't think of it as entertaining. Moving, intriguing, uplifting, thought-provoking – yes. Emotional, spiritual, intellectual too. Perhaps also contemplative, dreamlike, absorbing. But 'entertainment' seemed wide of the mark, and when I mentioned it to musician friends afterwards, they all said they would have felt the same.

Yet over the centuries, and back in the good old days when popular and 'art' music inhabited the same universe, musicians have been entertainers more often than not. Employed at court or by wealthy patrons to provide soothing background music, musicians of earlier centuries would have been used to being ignored or only half-heard (though Mozart as a child had the confidence to demand silence when he played the piano). In public performances, silence was not expected from the audience. Only the fortunate few would get to entertain their masters in private where, as we learn from Shakespeare, a well-chosen song could be the catalyst for someone's new train of thought.

But often musicians, even when public concerts and opera performances became popular, had to accept that the audience would chat, move about, drink and play cards. Mozart was pleased one night in the 1780s when the Emperor, 'against his usual habit', stayed for the whole of the concert. A century later, when Clara Schumann visited London to give a chamber-music concert, a critic commented that the playing was so majestic that 'the majority of the audience stayed until the end'. If this was unusual enough to provoke comment from a newspaper, musicians must have had a nerve-racking time of it.

So when did concerts become something to pay close attention to, in silence? It's a change that seems to have happened gradually, and undoubtedly has a complex explanation. The change may have been accelerated by the two World Wars, which changed people's view of life and of their leaders, leading to a perception that art – especially music – had the power to console, uplift, provide escape. It may also have something to do with the decreasing popularity of formal religion in the West. For many of my friends, art has a quasi-religious status in their lives. I don't mean that they worship it, but that they look principally to music, painting and literature for spiritual meaning or illumination. They find artistic insights as profoundly meaningful as those offered by religion or philosophy. Creative artists sense this search for illumination and try their best to provide it. Interpreters try to bring those spiritual qualities alive.

And so for many players and listeners, concerts are a serious activity. Audiences don't only want musicians to play well. They also hope for an extra dimension which takes them into new realms of reflection and meaning and, judging from what they say afterwards, many people find in classical music what they're looking for. However, as artists have come to feel that their task is important, so audiences find their behaviour under review. Early in the twentieth century the pianists Rachmaninov and Cortot refused to begin if there was noise and distraction in the hall. Sir Thomas Beecham was admired for refusing to start an orchestral concert until the audience had stopped coughing and fidgeting. For years now, major concert halls have routinely placed requests in the programme booklet for coughs and sneezes to be stifled. Mitsuko Uchida stopped in the middle of a Wigmore Hall recital because mobile phones were disturbing her. András Schiff walked off stage in Israel for the same reason, returning to give the audience an earnest speech about 'the terrorism of noise'. Steven Isserlis wrote in the *Guardian* about the unacceptable distraction of people coughing and nodding off in his line of vision. Even with a beautifully behaved Japanese audience, I have come close to asking the hall manager to make a plea for less uninhibited coughing after the interval. Clearly we players feel that silence is the only context in which our playing can blossom.

There are many different kinds of music in the world, and each has its own type of performance as well as its own type of audience. Some kinds of music are designed to entertain, but many have performers and listeners who are utterly serious about them. And each type of performance has its own code of behaviour. This is often overlooked when people are discussing the quiet atmosphere of classical concerts.

People speak of classical concerts as though they are unique in demanding certain behaviour from their audiences, but many kinds of music do the same. Jazz clubs and pop concerts have their own rituals, which have to be learned by the listeners. At a jazz club, for example, it's offensive if you don't clap to show your appreciation at the end of a fine solo during a longer piece, just as it's offensive at a classical concert if you do. At pop concerts it's de rigueur to burst into applause as soon as you recognise the start of a song, thus obliterating its opening bars.

It is true that classical concerts feel different because of the silence that reigns in the audience. Other kinds of music often take place against a background of audience talk and movement, but we classical performers hope for stillness. One reason is that we are among the few types of musicians today who don't use amplification when we play. Many musicians in other genres take it for granted. Against their high levels of amplified sound, the murmur of audience noise is much less distracting for them than it is for us. We are very aware that the fine gradations of tone, over which we labour so much in rehearsal, will not be heard if there is noise and movement in the hall.

But this is only part of it. We feel that the level at which music is played and broadcast these days has become overwhelming. Music, especially pop, is delivered to us at all hours of the day in public spaces and at a volume we have no way of controlling. People who go to such concerts give up the idea of talking to their companions, because there is no way of making themselves heard. After we had played a recent concert in Memphis, we went down to the famous Beale Street to hear a well-known blues group. The amplified noise level was so staggering that afterwards a couple of our party said they had wondered if they were having a heart attack. In a sense it felt as though amplification was the real event, and the music was mainly a vehicle for shattering noise levels to be delivered to a sensation-hungry audience.

For us it is the opposite. Our instruments are made of wood, often hundreds of years old, and we like their natural sound in the room. We also like the natural balance between different instruments, and we work hard on getting the balance just right. Amplification would distort all of that. We want people to hear acoustic instruments resonating in the room as they truly do. But this too is only a part of why we appreciate silence. Our need for quiet attention has grown in proportion to the feeling that the noise level is rising around us. Loud music is everywhere these days, and people pay very little attention to it. We want to move in the opposite direction. We want music to be acoustically natural, to be finely graded, to be worth stopping everything else for. We want the performance to be a special event. The silence that has become characteristic of classical concerts is helpful, but it is probably also defensive. It's a voluntary response of all concerned to an environment bursting with meaningless noise. Classical musicians of the past probably didn't require so much silence, because they were not competing against so much noise.

The rapt attention that is given to classical performances is loved by some and resented by others. Some say that classical music has become stuffy and rigid, or that they don't like coming to our concerts because they have to sit quietly. But others would say that this kind of music, thoughtfully played and listened to, is a highlight of their lives. Classical music has undoubtedly become more serious than it once was, in direct correlation with the rise of the entertainment industry, which focuses of course on pop. Now here is music specifically designed to entertain. And it's fantastically successful. It's also based on an elaborate pretence. Whole careers are based on people not being who they really are, not saying what they really think, and not looking as they naturally look. In fact, some of the stars admit that they can't sing or play the instruments we 'see' them playing. 'I'm crap', boasted Victoria Beckham in a newspaper headline. We are bludgeoned into overlooking all this pretence and accepting the premise that music is merely an entertainment. The richest, most successful musicians in the world are entertainers and proud of it.

Mozart described going to a fair shortly after his opera *The Marriage of Figaro* was first produced. Already there were hurdy-gurdies cranking out his arias, to his and everyone else's delight. He was no doubt pleased to be entertaining people as well as satisfying their deepest musical needs. But he was lucky to be living at a time before deep divisions had sprung up between popular and serious music. If someone thanked him for entertaining them, he probably didn't feel belittled. Indeed, he wrote to his father that he was glad his music appealed both to the ordinary punter and to the cognoscenti. But today, music is far more divided. Classical artists are conscious that they are not part of the entertainment industry; they want and need to provide something very different. They know that listeners often turn to classical music as a refuge from meaningless noise elsewhere. All this makes our task feel rather different from that of the musicians of Mozart's time. We feel we're guarding a material that becomes more and more precious, and perhaps more and more fragile, as time goes on. Is this why we don't really want to be classed as entertainers?

F is for Formula

A year or two ago, many musicians were struck by news reports that the councillors of Stoke-on-Trent were playing records of Beethoven's Ninth Symphony in the shopping centre to deter 'undesirables' from hanging around after hours. They gleefully reported that the troublesome youths just didn't want to be there any more. What did this say about the music? Did they mean that classical music is actually repellent, makes people want to be somewhere else? Or was the meaning benign: that a piece like the Ninth Symphony would create a serious, disciplined atmosphere, in which the urge to shout and break things would just ebb away?

This same symphony has been used by American leadership gurus to encourage groups of managers to bond and create dynamic motivational energy. During a long weekend, participants learn to sing the famous 'Ode to Joy' which comes in the final movement. The climactic moment of the seminar occurs when they sing it in chorus, sometimes even in a concert hall with an orchestra, finding a new sense of purpose and team spirit as they do so. When I think of Beethoven blaring out from Stoke city centre, therefore, I imagine a wave of repelled hooligans bursting out of the shopping mall, only to collide with an incoming wave of inspired managers surfing towards the music that brought them together. Another image, that of Malcolm McDowell and his henchmen running amok to the sound of the same symphony in the film of *A Clockwork Orange*, hints that crowd dispersal may not be the only effect of this astonishingly multifaceted music. The ancient Greeks told us that you can get people into any sort of mood you want by playing them the right sort of music, and modern-day military commanders have confirmed this. However, it is difficult to predict what great music will do to listeners' moods. Will they advance? Retreat? Mow down the innocent populace, sweep them up in a paean of loving kindness?

Since the Stoke story first appeared, there have been several similar reports. A bus station in the north of England discovered the repellent power of Vivaldi. Managers noted approvingly that troublemakers made themselves scarce when the concourse was flooded with baroque concertos. This was even more puzzling. Beethoven might seem a bit threatening, but surely Vivaldi is the essence of easy-going cheer? Then came further reports about city-centre locations where the authorities were using Mozart, and Italian opera arias sung by Pavarotti, as a means of teen-cleansing. Teenagers, allegedly, do not want to be seen in any place where the music is 'so uncool'. As a musician I feel offended by this, though I realise that it is not a comment on the music itself, but on what it represents to that age-group. The music of Mozart is constantly cited by scientists as encouraging growth in plants, intelligence in unborn babies, milk yield in cows, and concentration in school classrooms. That it should have the opposite effect on teenagers is not to do with its content but rather with theirs. Music, specifically pop music, has become a statement about tribal allegiance.

Classical music is fighting to keep its niche in the public's awareness. Classical record companies are in trouble and so are their artists. The annual *Gramophone* Awards have reinvented themselves, focusing on celebrities and getting rid of all those little specialist categories so hard to publicise. The Royal Philharmonic Society has followed suit and rolled several of its award categories into one, cutting down on prizes. And John Humphrys, interviewing the Proms Controller on Radio 4's *Today* programme, asks him what it's like to run a festival of classical music at a time when audiences are dwindling.

It's a fact, though, that classical music has never enjoyed mass popularity. As a schoolchild I was in a small minority because I liked classical music, and the same is true of schools today. Now we have a new generation which has not only grown up with pop music but has been force-fed it by hugely powerful media outlets, to the obliteration of practically all other kinds of music. Pop is no longer simply a form of entertainment, but a phenomenon that goes way beyond music to define the identity of the young. In the course of doing so it has marginalised many other forms of music which now feel genuinely threatened. Pop is so universally played, so available, so cleverly marketed and so idolised by a generation with money to buy records on a weekly basis that to like pop is to be young, and to be young is to like pop music. The music itself is almost secondary, but even top politicians like to jump on the bandwagon, as Tony Blair did when he said, 'I haven't come to classical music yet – I like what the kids like.' Probably no previous prime minister has either felt that way or – more pertinently – thought it wise to say he feels that way.

No other form of music has ever had this power. However, what really puzzles a music-lover is that pop's rise to world dominance coincides with a poverty of invention that makes this generation of pop maybe the dullest music we've ever had. You need only spend one evening listening to any pop radio station across the world to know that most songwriters in all countries now work to a formula. The same disco beat, the same tiny short phrases, timid harmonies, melodies culled from just two or three notes, real instruments replaced by electronic sounds, performers who can't even sing. Compared with the popular music of any other decade I can think of, today's surely has the least to offer a music-lover. It's 'feelgood music' without either feeling or being good.

More and more people are waking up to the effects of globalisation. Organised protests focus on the serious effects of capitalism, but individual protesters often add that they don't want to have products like Coke and McDonald's forced on them in every corner of the globe. Pop music is another example of globalisation. It's ruthlessly exported all over the world, not to improve the quality of our lives but simply as a means of making megabucks for the big companies who produce it. It squeezes out local variation and individual expression. Pop is the music of capitalism, 'a cruel and shallow money trench, a long plastic hallway where thieves and pimps run free and good men die like dogs', as Louis Barfe said in his recent survey of the industry.* In order for its bosses to make really big money, we all have to be listening to the same thing. And we have

* *Where Have All the Good Times Gone?: The Rise and Fall of the Record Industry* (Atlantic, 2004)

to buy the idea that each new song self-destructs after a week, that next Saturday we'll need to buy the next one. Amazingly, we do. Only last for a week? What a contrast with the composers of the past, who hoped for their music to last for years and years and years!

People need to wake up to the narrow diet of music they're being fed by commercial record companies. We need an equivalent of the delightful campaign begun in Italy to promote what they call 'Slow Food'; not just slow music, obviously, but real music. The Slow Food advocates want to bring back local variation, ancient expertise, garden herbs, individuality, conversation. Make people realise it's not an advance in society to be able to buy the same synthetic lunch in Algiers or Alaska. In musical terms, we should make people realise that they don't want to clean their teeth to the same ten chart-toppers pumping out of their radios twenty-four hours a day from Barcelona to Beijing. Don't get me wrong: a well-made hamburger with good ingredients can be a delicious meal. A cheap imitation full of E-numbered chemicals is an insult to the original dish. In the same way, a great popular song can be a joy for ever. But a cynical, manipulative sham just leaves your ear hungry for the real thing. Good music, like good food, needs to taste of something, not just make you feel the same as every other consumer. We don't need synthetic moods to be created by music; we want to hear music that expresses all the facets of human experience and feelings. Let that be in any musical genre – as long as it's not formulaic, but personal and genuine, as the popular music of the past used to be.

A piece like Beethoven's Ninth, which has lasted for generations, was not written to a formula or to create one simple mood. It expresses a huge range of hopes and feelings, and was meant to be a treasury of them for years to come. That's why it can never be successfully used, as pop music is used, to make large numbers of people behave in the same way. It may make them dream, or go home in a thoughtful mood, or feel energetic and happy, and it may even draw them towards the city centre. But whatever effect it has, it won't be fast, cheap or predictable.

G is for Grace

Grace is a word often encountered in music. From the little ornaments known as grace notes to the graceful movements which are often spoken about by teachers and listeners, and to the feeling of grace that sometimes descends on a performer, the concept is never far away.

The grace of a player's movements is often described in accounts of listening to music. From the exquisite descriptions of eleventh-century Japanese courtesans entertaining their visitors with samisen music in *The Tale of Genji*, through the nubile elegance of Jane Austen heroines delighting their audience (or not) on the pianoforte, grace and playing an instrument clearly go together in many people's minds. It seems to be associated primarily with women, but not exclusively; the elegance of a musician's physical movement can be part of any artist's charm. Yet it's a word that's difficult to take as a compliment, because it seems to imply music as a social accomplishment rather than as a powerful means of expression. To be called 'graceful' implies that the player is conscious of their movements around the instrument, their arm movements in the air. These, one feels, could be practised in front of a mirror without actually making any sound on the instrument itself. It is the body language that is important, and designed to produce an effect on the onlooker.

These days, gracefulness has waned as a paramount ingredient in playing an instrument. This change must follow other social changes, as well as changes in attitudes towards music. Both sexes now earn their living as musicians, and playing an instrument is no longer a means of displaying your gentleness and fragility to prospective suitors. On the contrary, it is now important to show that you are a force to be reckoned with, worth the money that your listeners have paid for their tickets. Expressive power is now desirable both from men and women, and indeed it often seems that the more powerful, the less graceful a player is, or wants to be. Not only that, but the volume has increased. Concert halls are larger, instruments are set up to be able to produce louder sounds than before, and more physical strength is needed to play them. It would not be possible to get the full range of tone out of the modern Steinway piano or the violin with modern steel strings if one used only the minimal movements of the Jane Austen-era musician. A new repertoire of movements, those of the emotionally charged interpreter, has become fascinating to audiences and players alike. Strength and control are prized more highly than grace. Indeed, a player who is predominantly graceful may be perceived as having a limited range of tone.

In the last few decades there has sprung up a small industry of physiotherapists who minister to the many players with aches and pains. Many orchestras have in-house doctors and therapists. As the emphasis on big tone and large-scale expression has grown, so has the array of physical problems associated with making them. The more involved players feel, the more they put their bodies under pressure. In former times it would have been considered unattractive to sweat with exertion at an instrument, but the pendulum has now swung almost the other way: unless you can demonstrate serious physical effort, your artistry won't be believed. The player who walks off the platform cool as a cucumber is probably heartless, and nobody can make a career like that. In the course of developing intensity in their playing, many people get literally in a twist. Therefore many therapists are employed to try to show musicians how to relax, how to use their muscles correctly, how to avoid stress, and how to find points of balance which they do not allow themselves to abandon in the heat of the moment.

This has mixed results. People become focused on playing without pain. On the face of it, this may seem a reasonable goal, but thinking about physical well-being doesn't always go along with musical involvement. It often seems to mean that the player doesn't engage with the instrument enough to get the full range of expression out of it. In my experience, many players who have learned to avoid pain triggers are also less expressive as a result; as the German proverb says, 'Beauty has to suffer.' There are a few talented souls who can be relaxed, pain-free and powerfully expressive at the same time, but most people have to choose between comfort and effectiveness.

All those with wide experience of performing eventually encounter 'grace' in another sense. It describes the feeling you get when you realise that your own powers are limited, or not under your control, and yet you suddenly gain access to greater mastery than you were aware of possessing. In a recent talk for a London music club, Janet Baker spoke of the feeling that sometimes descends over a group of musicians, even though they may be repeating something for the umpteenth time in a rehearsal or recording session. Suddenly, something changes and everyone becomes aware that they are operating at a new level of intensity or shared communication. Ethnomusicologists have just begun to explore the phenomenon of 'entrainment', a scientific term for the process whereby groups of people (or even objects such as pendulums) start to synchronise their movements or their body clocks. It seems that the phenomenon may apply to music-making as well, or at least have echoes in the way that people play together. People sharing a musical activity can develop more than predictable intuitions, and they may have the feeling of developing extra powers as well. 'Powers' is not quite the right word, for an essential quality of this feeling of grace is that it just arrives, whether you have earned it or not.

It is not necessary, however, to belong to a group to have the feeling of the sudden magnification of one's powers. Indeed, I could not say whether I had experienced it more often when alone or when playing with others. I suspect, also, that I have sometimes felt it in a group situation where others did not experience it (and no doubt they would say that they had experienced it also when I did not). It may be partly influenced by others' participation, but the feeling is not necessarily shared. This is not entrainment, but perhaps its opposite: the sense of being individually blessed.

Sometimes players feel that they have done all the necessary practice, but their performance fails to catch light. At other times, for no apparent reason, a player may suddenly feel that they have access to a new level of mastery over themselves and the instrument. This feeling is often unrelated to the outer circumstances. For example, it can occur in the most unpromising halls and when one is tired or out of sorts. Conversely, it can fail to occur on important occasions when you really wish it would happen. It seems not to have a physiological basis. It isn't the cumulative result of lots and lots of practising; it may be, but it certainly isn't a result one can calculate. People may think of it in different ways, but we might all agree to call it some kind of grace, or unforeseen access to a sphere in which one is unusually bonded with the music and the means of making it come alive.

'Grace' is often used with a religious connotation, but that is not what I mean here, or at least not specifically. Some musicians may identify it with godliness, but many others will feel it as an unmerited glimpse of effortlessness. No musician is likely to think that they caused it by some cleverness of their own. They have the feeling of being helped, not perhaps by a definable agency, but helped nonetheless to climb higher in the tower of consciousness, and to look out over a wider horizon. For these moments one can only be grateful. Indeed, those who don't know how to feel grateful probably don't experience those moments in the first place.

H is for Hands

I often look down at my fingers and wonder what evolutionists have to say about hands and their ability to play music. Hands, we are told, evolved in such a way that we could oppose fingers and thumbs in order to pick things up and hold them. Primates can sort seeds, comb through fur, hang on to branches, catch small prey. When scientists talk about how far our manual skills have developed since we evolved into humans, there are often joking references to monkeys learning to type, as though typing were the antithesis of the usual things that monkeys do with their hands, an example of extraordinary digital skill way beyond the dreams of furry animals.

Typing is undoubtedly a skill, and a very useful one, but the manual skill needed to play Chopin studies on the piano, or Beethoven's Violin Concerto, is of quite a different order. Who would ever have thought that with only five fingers on each hand, a person could weave the magic tapestry of fingerwork demanded by our favourite virtuoso music? Who would have thought, indeed, that it would ever occur to us to use hands in this way? The speed and accuracy required, the finesse of touch and judgement, are not strictly necessary for survival. Hands are important in all the arts, either for wielding tools or for expression, but in the playing of instrumental music, hands have entered into a new realm of achievement.

And yet hands themselves continue to look very ordinary. The ability to play *The Flight of the Bumble Bee* on an instrument, or to improvise at lightning speed, does not hone the fingers into gorgeous tapers. When musicians' hands are at rest, you would never know by looking at them that they possess amazing powers. Quite often people come up to me after concerts and say things like, 'Let me look at your hands.' And then they take my hands and look vaguely dissatisfied. My hands do not look and feel as if they have been anywhere near the refining fire of the arts.

All through my playing career, members of audiences have said to me, 'I hope you have insured your hands!' They're dismayed to hear that I haven't, but in fact I don't know anyone who has, unless my colleagues are keeping the fact quiet. I think most of us instinctively feel that if we were to treat our hands as fragile objects, daily life would become unbearably fraught. An early piano teacher of mine was full of little warnings and superstitions about hands. Don't play tennis; don't do the washing-up before you practise, don't use sharp knives, don't carry heavy things. Don't wear a watch when you practise because it makes one wrist heavier than the other. Don't cut your nails on the day of a concert because it makes your hands 'feel different'. Don't put on hand cream because it changes the tactile relationship between the keys and the skin of your fingers. Even as a child, I felt that this pointed to a lifetime of vigilance not guaranteed to make me a better person or a finer musician.

Actually, I suspect I have a sort of counter-intuitively risky approach to sharp knives and hot ovens, as though I want to prove to myself that I am not living in an ivory tower (an image especially apt for pianists). I probably cut myself more than other members of the household do when chopping vegetables. I'm still being teased about the day I plunged my hand into a casserole full of popping popcorn and stirred it around, with the result that I had to play several concerts with three fingers in bandages. I don't think I'm especially clumsy; it's something to do with needing to know that I have not become precious and neurotic about my hands.

Is everyone born with the capacity to use their hands in the skilful way that instrumentalists do, or are there only certain people who have the raw material? Even amongst musicians it sometimes seems that there is a certain type of manual cleverness possessed only by the subset of musicians who are instrumentalists. We all know people who are good musicians, but not good players. They may be superb composers, teachers, conductors, and gifted listeners. But they never develop executant skill on an instrument. Their brains are willing, but their hands are weak. Actually, dexterity can be very specific; there are people who are 'naturals' on one instrument but not on another. I, for example, always found it natural to play the piano, but had to wrestle with the violin to reach a level good enough to allow me to play in junior and student orchestras. Conversely, I have friends who are great string players, but quite ham-fisted on the piano. It seems that hands have likes and dislikes.

Whether a player's hand is large or small does not necessarily produce a predictable result. Often people with small hands, myself included, shy away from repertoire which requires them to stretch intervals more than they can naturally encompass. For example, I have a physical dislike of playing pieces that constantly ask me to stretch more than an octave, my natural limit. But there are pianists with small hands who nevertheless tackle and manage to master pieces written by or for someone with much bigger hands. They somehow find a way to refine their lateral movement so that they can rotate the hand, fast enough to cover a big space. Conversely, great big bears of Russian pianists can produce miracles of deftness and speed, although their hands look as if they could wield nothing more delicate than a cleaver. Pianist Vladimir Horowitz famously used a 'flat hand' technique which somehow didn't prevent him from being able to control the keys at lightning speed. Power is not predictable, either. Hungarian violinist Sándor Végh used to say that the biggest violin tone he ever heard was produced by a slim young woman, the French violinist Ginette Neveu. She was not conventionally strong; it was her wonderfully calibrated application of weight and pressure that produced something more penetrating than brute strength ever could.

I have sometimes wondered whether very specific instances of talent have anything to do with what I might call the latitude and longitude of playing particular instruments, or the dimensions that they require you to master. Think of the different ways in which instruments represent low to high notes. You could say that they correspond to width, depth and height. On the piano, the notes are in a lateral plane, running horizontally from 'low' on the left to 'high' on the right. On the violin, however, the fingerboard lies at right angles to that lateral plane, or at right angles to the body. To play high notes, you bring your hand closer to your face; for low notes you extend the hand away from you.

The fingerboard of the cello presents a third possibility. In its playing position the cello lies parallel with the trunk of the player's body. On any given string, the hand is close to your head for low notes, and moves towards your feet to produce high notes. 'Up' in pitch actually means 'down' in the accepted sense. High notes on the violin are closer to your head; on the cello 'high' means towards your feet. On most keyboard instruments, 'high' means away from the body to the right. The accordion, however, puts the keyboard in the longitudinal position, and 'high' means towards the floor. And for a harpist, 'high' means at the end of your arm's reach, arm held straight out in front. None of these versions of 'high' corresponds with how we usually refer to high – that is, towards the sky. Only some wind instruments, perhaps, have their high notes located physically higher, in the column of the oboe, recorder, clarinet. Otherwise, I can't think of an instrument whose high notes are produced by raising the hand in a conventionally upward direction. This means that musical instruments propose various spatial representations of low and high, almost all at variance with our everyday use of those terms.

Would it be foolish to speculate that manual comfort on a particular instrument may have something to do with one's spatial sense, with one's ability to master the plane on which the instrument requires the player to operate? Can it be that the sense of balance, for example, plays a role? I wonder, too, if even things like the sense of privacy, the sensitivity to personal space, are relevant. For a pianist, for example, the very size of the keyboard, and indeed of the whole instrument, guarantees them a certain amount of distance from the next player. Do some people need to sit down? Do others need to have their fingers close to their eyes? Is the material of the instrument important: do some hands get addicted to sliding over wood, while others need the cool touch of ivory? Are strings an important part of the tactile experience? Do some players get special satisfaction from operating in two planes at once, as all string players have to do if they use a bow? Are others undone by that same challenge? Is it physically helpful for some to have the notes of their instrument spread out across a wide area, and for others to have them all confined in a working space of six inches?

When you start learning to play an instrument, you are terribly aware of your hands. Instead of being the means of playing, they seem to be the barrier between you and the instrument. Why are they so slow, so dim, so unwilling to go where you want them to go? How can everyday life have been acceptable with such unsupple appendages? You find you have to learn movements you never needed before, and at speeds you didn't know could be achieved. As you become more adept, your hands start to be your servants. You enjoy the feeling of your hands on the instrument; your hands and the instrument start to feel bonded. And when you get to a really high level, your hands seem less and less crucial in your vision of yourself as a musician. Your imagination tells you what you want to hear, and instead of enquiring whether your hands will permit you to attempt this, you go straight to the desired result, hardly noticing how your hands achieve it. Your hands become a link in the chain between imagination and beautiful music sounding in the room. Yes, you need your hands to play an instrument, but ultimately it is the thought that counts.

I is for Instruments

'We could all be good musicians if it weren't for the fact that we have to play instruments,' said pianist György Sebök.

And it's tempting to leave this essay at that. Instruments, which should simply be the means through which we express ourselves, are often the means through which we don't. Instead of being extensions of our bodies and thoughts, instruments have a way of turning into obstacles between us and the music. Even singers, whose voices are part of them, would agree that they have to struggle to make their voices into the expressive instruments they want. Left to ourselves, we know just how we want the music to sound. We could sing it beautifully, or at least indicate it with effortless grace. But with a complicated lump of wood or metal in our hands, we suddenly become less expressive. We are preoccupied with how to make the instrument sound. It sometimes seems to control us, rather than us controlling it. At any rate, it seems to be a kind of gate between us and ideal music-making, opening and closing at random. When we listen to someone playing, it often seems that what we're primarily hearing is an exercise in playing the instrument, not an expression of music.

Instruments occupy an enormous amount of musicians' time, probably more than the music itself does. The act of being a musician is often the story of a long courtship with a particular instrument. Indeed, it is amazing how involved we get with our instruments, given the way that most of us choose them in the first place. I can think of a number of well-known musicians who had an instrument thrust into their hands at school by a music teacher desperate to add this or that instrument to the school wind band, brass band, or orchestra. Despite this random start, they willingly took on the challenge of their oboe or French horn, and years later are still spending hours and hours scraping bamboo, making reeds, tackling problems with embouchure (the position of the mouth on the instrument), even coping with dental work made necessary by prolonged pressure on the lips and teeth.

Equally, I know string players whose career started when they were more or less told to go into the school's instrument cupboard and pick out something to try in music lessons. Sometimes the choice was very limited. Despite their chance encounter with the cello or whatever, they willingly convert serendipity into destiny. In later years they may find themselves organising their whole finances around the attempt to purchase a really fine instrument, even compromising on a house purchase in order to have a satisfying cello. Now that string-instrument prices have matched those of fine art, top players often have to put together syndicates of investors to buy them an instrument they can never hope to own outright.

This can never happen to pianists, by the way, for generally speaking, pianos depreciate and deteriorate with age; the few that become collectors' pieces do so for reasons other than the sound. Pianos never attain the unique aura (or monetary value) of a Stradivari, Amati or Guarneri violin. If Steinway hired out top-flight concert violins instead of pianos, they wouldn't pension them off after about ten years; they wouldn't even start using them until they were two hundred years old. Pianists watch with mixed feelings the enormous efforts expended by string-playing friends to get hold of particular instruments, half-envious of the love affair they witness, but also relieved not to be caught up in this kind of obsession.

Quite apart from finance and the practical tasks of making or maintaining bits and pieces for the instrument, musicians become emotionally wedded to the instrument they play, even if they didn't consciously choose it in the first place. Often they and their instrument are known as a unit in their social circle: 'This is Bill – he's a guitarist,' 'Jill's a flute player.' A person and his or her instrument often seem to be locked in a long and complicated dance. They advance towards one another and retreat, sometimes insisting on space between them, sometimes entwined, but never breaking apart. Often – especially in the world of amateur music-making – the partnership continues long after the player has got as far as he or she is going to get with that particular instrument. But by then they have been moulded into 'a bassoonist' or 'a viola player' in the eyes of the musical community. It's most unusual for someone to give up and start another instrument from scratch, even if common sense might suggest that it would be a good idea. It's not just that a particular person plays the cello; they gradually become *a cellist*. Player and instrument become one being, just as man and horse were welded into the mythical centaur.

I still don't know what it was that made me gravitate towards the piano when I was a child. We didn't have any musical instruments in the house, so it can't have been the power of suggestion. Nobody told me I should try the piano. But there were pianos in some of my friends' houses, and eventually their parents mentioned to mine that I was playing the piano when I was over at their house. Had we ever thought of getting a piano? My parents mulled it over and decided to buy an upright, and by the time it arrived in our house I felt it was a relief to have one actually on the premises. Without knowing that I had wanted to play anything, it felt as though the piano had been missing. Years later I heard that my grandfather, who never had any musical instruction, was a nifty hand on the harmonium and accordion when he had the chance to play one. So perhaps the aptitude for a keyboard instrument was genetic. I can only say that the piano was 'my' instrument, and remained in top place despite my learning to play the violin and percussion instruments too. During my childhood and student years I actually had more fun with the violin and the percussion family, because they allowed me to join in the addictive social circle which is an orchestra. But unfortunately they never felt right in the same way that the piano did. I say 'unfortunately' because the life of a pianist is a good deal more isolated. That, too, was part of the player-plus-instrument bond that I didn't bargain for, but took on board in an enduring way.

On holiday recently in Italy, I managed to decipher an article about instruments in *La Stampa*. The writer said that he had been at a concert where a young prizewinning violinist had played a concerto on one of the most famous Stradivarius violins. During the performance, she broke a string and had the presence of mind to hand her violin to someone in the violin section. He handed her back his own violin, and she continued playing on that while the orchestral player changed the string on the Strad. What the journalist noticed was that, while obviously her technique and stage presence were identical, the actual sounds she produced on the two violins were quite different. The Strad had a glorious tone, and the borrowed instrument sounded muted, pale, as if the sun had gone behind a cloud. The writer mused on instruments and how we may need particular ones to reach our full potential. He wondered whether racing driver Michael Schumacher could be the fastest in the world if he didn't have the finest racing car in the world, and the finest team of mechanics to keep it in perfect condition. The players' skill can take them so far, he said, but if the instrument is limited, they will never achieve an ideal result. This view is borne out by the efforts of those who move heaven and earth to get hold of a particular violin. But I find it uncomfortable to think that someone can only be at their best on a perfect instrument. There's a definite hint of it playing them rather than them playing it; the violin's are the powers that are being harnessed.

In the world of sport, everyone takes it for granted that supreme achievement and supreme equipment go together. During the Olympics we hear a lot about the athletes' dependence on faultless equipment. If the tools are not perfect, a perfect score cannot be achieved, and often commentators say it's a shame that so-and-so was let down by the equipment. But after all, a sportsman is simply trying to be the fastest, jump the highest, be the most accurate, score the most goals. Someone like Michael Schumacher is not, as far as I know, hoping to express something beyond speed and superb control. But in the world of the arts, an instrument is the means through which an artist hopes to express something beyond control. And as usual in music, there are paradoxes when it comes to instruments.

There are players whose power of mind and character are such that they sound like themselves whatever instrument they're playing. Their characteristic way of handling it, the type of expression they employ, their timing, somehow transcend the limitations of the instrument. Anyone who's attended a public masterclass has probably heard an experienced teacher taking the instrument out of the student's hands and demonstrating that it can make sounds the student didn't know it could make. Some masters seem to relish this opportunity, while others shrink from using it because it can be so chastening for the student. I still remember an occasion when my trio was coaching a student trio, and our violinist took the instrument out of the student's hands and showed her how he would like her to play the passage we were discussing. He turned to hand her back the violin, and she was standing there with tears running down her face. We get so bonded with our instruments that it comes as a shock to hear that the sounds we make on them are not the only ones, or the best ones, that they can make.

Many successful performers become obsessed with a particular instrument. But great players also welcome the chance of showing that they can bend any instrument to their will. Perhaps the prime exponents of this mind-over-matter approach are pianists, who have to reconcile themselves to playing a different piano at every concert. The composer-pianist Ferruccio Busoni said that there were no bad pianos, only bad pianists. It is not true, of course, that there are no bad pianos; his remark alluded to the attitude necessary to overcome a bad instrument.

All musicians have to learn how to think beyond the instrument, pianists probably more than most because their instrument is such a daunting collection of mechanical parts. I felt quite offended when a piano technician first showed me a model of the working parts of the piano, all hammers, felts and levers. Irrationally I thought, 'That's nothing to do with how the sound of the piano is made.' When I touch the keys, I never think about the complicated mechanism that results in a hammer striking a string a couple of feet away. I imagine that the sound arises directly under my fingers. And like most pianists, I maintain that a sustained singing tone is possible on the piano, despite evidence that each note dies away from the moment it is struck. It's essential to think beyond the assemblage of hinges, sticks and felts; anyone who limits themselves to what the piano *seems* to be able to do will remain at a low level of artistic achievement, and indeed one sees this often enough in those 'bad pianists' about whom Busoni spoke.

The Russian pianist Sviatoslav Richter said that some of his best concerts were given on indifferent school pianos in the Russian provinces. Those instruments forced him to think about what was at the heart of the music. In other words, since there wasn't much that could be drawn out of the piano, he had to think beyond the instrument. He couldn't change the sound of the piano, but through the power of his imagination he could make the audience focus on other things – and they did. This was the musical equivalent of winning the Grand Prix on a clapped-out old banger – impossible in the sporting world, yet inspiringly possible in the arts. The jazz pianist Keith Jarrett, in a recent television documentary, recalled that his most famous recording, 'The Köln Concert', was made on the wrong piano. His chosen piano had failed to turn up; he played an inferior one that happened to be in the hall, and found that its drawbacks actually stimulated him to think new thoughts.

I attended concerts given by famous violinists – Yehudi Menuhin, Sándor Végh – in their later years, when their control of the instrument was less than it once had been. We all heard the scratches, the bow shaking, the notes out of tune. They would have been offensive in a player who couldn't think beyond the instrument, but with them it was just a kind of surface noise. Mysteriously, they were able to make the audience feel that the actual golden tone was of secondary importance. A gorgeous sound would have been a bonus, but we got the message anyway, for they were expressing something beyond speed and technical control. Like all musicians, they still had to play an instrument to express themselves, but in their hands it was just that: an instrument.

J is for Job (Not a Proper)

All my life I have been squeezed between the contradictory opinions of people divided on the topic of whether being a musician is, or is not, a proper job. Sometimes it seems as if musicians hold an elevated position in the hierarchy of jobs, and sometimes that they never even make it on to the bottom rung of the career ladder.

When I was a child, the overwhelming message I got from those around me was that I was lucky to have a talent for something. Biblical language was often used by adults to convince me that I should not hide my light under a bushel, or follow in the footsteps of the lazy son who was given some coins (poignantly identified as 'talents') by his father and who, alone among his brothers, did nothing more enterprising than dig a hole and put the money in the ground for safe keeping. It was often put to me that it would be wasteful and selfish not to make the most of my musical aptitude. If you had a 'gift from God' you shouldn't turn the other cheek.

As soon as I turned professional, however, I found that the outside world regarded music as a deeply suspect choice of career. Many people seemed to think it self-indulgent to be a musician. The long childhood training suddenly seemed as if it had only been preparation for a hobby, for clearly music was not real work. Did we musicians think we could do something we loved, and would have done for pleasure anyway, and be paid for it? Looking around me, I realised that many people did not love what they were doing from 9 a.m. to 5 p.m. They accepted that boredom and routine were their only way of getting their hands on a reliable pay-packet. They thought it was just greedy of musicians to expect an income from something which actually gave them pleasure. When I first complained about the hardships of the freelance music world, friends told me sourly, 'Well, at least you like doing what you do.' It was generally held that there was an inverse relationship between liking what you did and being remunerated for it. I was tricked into thinking that lousy income was a small price to pay for interesting nine-to-five activity.

Most of my colleagues had been buffeted by extremely mixed advice about music as a profession. Generally speaking, they had been mightily encouraged and showered with praise all through their musical childhoods, singled out in their peer groups because of their talent. They had got up early and stayed up late for years and years in order to practise. Their families had spent handsome sums on their music lessons and their instruments. They had given up all kinds of social opportunities because of the demands of music lessons and concerts. And all this was assumed to be leading up to something special. Other children might have things they intended to do, but gifted young musicians had destinies. Making career decisions was too mundane for people whose musical talent would enable them to fly over the heads of their contemporaries as if on a magic carpet.

And yet when it came to making decisions about jobs and careers, the music-lovers of the family were elbowed out of the limelight by the economists. When money became an issue, a career in music was suddenly much less desirable. Fathers who had backed their talented offspring all the way through grade exams and music competitions were suddenly aghast at the idea of those same youngsters trying to earn a living from music. In those days before equal opportunities, boys were hit especially hard. People assumed that boys would become responsible for the income of their family, and the armchair economists knew that music was not the source of a steady income. After being shown off as young players, boys were suddenly told that music was best kept as a hobby. Girls were told that if they persisted in being musicians they would have to find a husband willing to support their non-lucrative choice of career. None of this had been mentioned during all the years of practice and dedication.

Of course, every society has its own view of what a proper job is, and the obvious question is: why is music not a proper job? Music carries some of humanity's finest impulses and spiritual expressions, and contributes to society's psychological health, so it should be worth more than many other endeavours. The question of whether it is a proper job has a different flavour in different countries. In Britain, no artist is considered to have a proper job. Most parents would experience a tremor of anxiety if their offspring announced they were marrying an actor, painter, poet, folk singer. But if our society regarded these jobs as valuable, they would be better funded and better paid, becoming 'proper' in the process. In Britain a proper job means regular hours and reliable pay. Better still, you should be seen to be at work, seen by people around you in the same position; having a proper job contains a large element of fitting in.

If you laze around at home and occasionally produce something that earns lots of money, that's not a proper job. If you work extremely hard and make almost nothing, that's not a proper job either. A poet who labours for weeks over a poem and wins a £50 prize cannot congratulate themself on finally having a proper job. If that same poet writes a film script that wins an Oscar, is that more proper? Is being Leonardo da Vinci a proper job? Is it more of a proper job to be Leonardo than to be Damien Hirst? Is being a supermodel a proper job, earning thousands of pounds each week? Is working in a Far Eastern sweatshop a proper job? Even the notion of a proper job may be under attack, now that many jobs are losing their security.

When I started off as a young professional musician, concert offers were slow to materialise. I sometimes 'temped' as a secretary because my keyboard skills had enabled me to become a fast typist. These were the only times in my life when I worked predictable hours in someone else's office. I could not get over the empty feeling of spending eight hours a day typing someone else's letters, filing someone else's forms. Nothing I produced would be my work or credited to me, not even if I became a permanent staff member. My bosses would thank me for doing something quickly, but I didn't originate anything, influence what was said, or see the result of what I was involved in. Every day I came out at 5 p.m. feeling as if my own mind had been 'on hold'. I felt as if I hadn't yet begun work for that day, which was just as well, considering that I still had to practise my piano in the evening. Yet friends were impressed that I was actually engaging with the world of work. Was this the proper job that society would have preferred me to do?

I was used to spending the day practising, rehearsing, studying, memorising music, doing my own admin, trying to create concert opportunities (all unpaid). On concert days, I would work late into the night. My glimpse of office life was unsettling. I knew that any competent person could have done what I did there. In other words, I and any other competent person were interchangeable: *it didn't have to be me*. This was not something I had ever felt in the world of music. Nevertheless, as a secretary I was paid by the hour whether I was doing anything useful or not. Being brilliant wouldn't earn me more pay, but I couldn't be paid less either. If there was no work to be done, I was paid anyway. And at certain times it was taken for granted that we wouldn't tackle anything new, but would just tidy our desks, hang around chatting, and wait for the moment we could leave.

This was all utterly different from life as a musician. I spent long hours practising the piano, for which I was not paid. When I joined a chamber group, we spent enormous amounts of time rehearsing, and enormous amounts of time writing letters, researching opportunities and making phone calls to drum up work. That was unpaid too. When we finally got concert offers, we were usually paid for the concerts, but the fees had retrospectively to cover all the unpaid time that we had spent practising and rehearsing. On paper the concert fees looked fine, but they never covered all the time and effort spent in getting and preparing for the concert, trying to publicise it, buying music, travelling across the city to rehearsals, buying concert clothes and accessories, maintaining instruments, travelling to the concert itself, staying overnight if it was far from London, and paying commission to any concert agent who had been involved. A large part of what we earned had immediately to be deducted for expenses. I felt this keenly when applying for my first bank loan. My bank manager looked through my accounts and pointed out that his young secretary earned the same as I did, but that she was considerably richer in real terms because she had no expenses, whereas I had to spend about a third of my total income on financing my work (and therefore should not be lent a large sum of money).

When we in the chamber group compared our lives with those of more sensible friends who had gone into, say, the Civil Service or accountancy, our position seemed foolhardy. If we did not get concerts, there would be no money. The satisfaction that we got from a successful concert would be offset by the worry of weeks without income until the next one. There was no sickness benefit, no paid holidays, no pension. No tenure, no subsidised canteen, no company car, no maternity leave, no sabbaticals. Clearly it was far from being a proper job. And yet we remained dedicated musicians, still fuelled by the years of preparation that brought us to this point. In a pre-industrial society we might have found a happier place, with people around us making things and getting paid erratic prices for them, or not making things and not getting paid. If everyone around us were responsible for their own handiwork, living on the proceeds of what they could grow or produce, seeing the immediate result of their labours, we might fit in better. As it is, being a freelance musician probably hasn't changed very much for centuries, whereas many other jobs have changed beyond recognition. I used to think that having a wildly fluctuating income, dependent on one's own enterprise, was an intriguing and – how shall I put it? – a *lifelike* way of proceeding. However, as the years went on I noticed that other people on their boringly inert salaries had achieved far greater material ease.

These days, when we meet freelance musicians from other countries, we often compare notes. They face similar problems, but we envy them in at least one important respect. Many foreign musicians – especially from mainland Europe and Scandinavia – thrive on the knowledge that their work is considered important. Musicians have high status in the community, even if they are not rich, and their vocation is regarded as a higher calling than a mere 'proper job'. The luckiest ones are supported with all manner of grants, residencies and rewards unavailable in this country. Here, the status of musicians is equivocal. People are happy to come and applaud at concerts while breathing a sigh of relief that they are not married to a musician. Musicians themselves regard their work as culturally important, but wish it were equally valued by the community. And as for enrichment and reward, these remain largely metaphorical.

K is for Keeping Emotions out of Music

Last week a friend wrote to say that she was going to sing at the funeral of a relative. 'I can't imagine how I'll do it without crying,' she said. She wondered if it is hard for professional musicians to play sad music in public – do they have to feel sad too? Or do they have to shut themselves off from the emotion of the music in order to be able to perform?

Players of jazz, Indian raga, and Western classical music might all give different answers. However, all kinds of musicians grapple with the same problem; if the voice breaks then the tone cannot be controlled, and what the listener hears is you rather than the music. In instrumental music there are equivalents of the voice breaking: trembling limbs, nerves, memory problems, poor breathing, self-absorption, obsession with appearance. All these can interfere between the musician and the music, and between the music and the listener. Some of the most outwardly emotional music requires enormous control from the performers. In Spain recently I saw a performance of flamenco. On the surface it couldn't have been more fervent, but at the same time one could feel the rigorous control and finesse of all the performers. It was very expressive, but never randomly so. Clearly these 'hot' performers kept a cool head.

Classical performers have to strike a balance between presenting themselves and presenting the composer's work.

To deliver the music with its own meaning intact, it seems that players have to remain separate from it, or at least enough to control it. They have to use their own experience to understand the composer, but they mustn't *identify* with the emotion of the music, or (paradoxically) it will be diminished. It's dangerous to think you know everything the composer means. There may be more in the music than the performer has decided to express, or is capable of expressing.

Years ago I was very struck by André Previn describing a concert in which he conducted a Romantic symphony immediately after hearing that a close friend had died. Feeling distraught, he resolved to dedicate the performance of the symphony to his friend's memory. Throughout the piece he felt convinced that a sense of tragic power had elevated the whole performance. However, when he watched a video of the concert afterwards, he was horrified to find that far from raising the level of the performance, his misery had got in the way. The way he directed the orchestra seemed haphazard and melodramatic, and his facial expressions distracting. His emotional identification with the music had actually prevented him from controlling it.

Musicians can't understand music without using their emotional intelligence, and indeed it is this that dictates the shape and timing of their performances, making one player meaningfully different from another. But they also have to learn how to use their emotions as a lens through which to see and let things be seen. As Daniel Barenboim once said in a televised masterclass, 'Your task is to convey the emotion, not to experience it!' Some may think that learning to put your own feelings on hold is nothing extraordinary. After all, people in all walks of life have to do it every day in order to get on with their work. But in most professions, work is not about communicating emotion. If someone in an office hides their feelings, that's the end of the matter; feelings are not conveyed. In the arts, however, to work is to bring emotions alive. Nobody can do that in a state of emotional numbness. If an artist wholly suppresses his or her feelings, music may not be conveyed.

As I don't witness my performances, I couldn't say whether I successfully keep my personal worries off the concert stage. But when I listen to my recordings, I'm often surprised that my emotional state isn't detectable on them. (Of course they are 'only' sound recordings, and collect no visual evidence.) Recording is very stressful, and people's nerves are sometimes screwed really tight. In recording sessions I have had all sorts of problems that I thought were going to ruin the result. Recently, for example, there was a problem with the piano I had chosen. Midway through the record I had to abandon it and change to a different instrument. The hours of strain and ill-tempered discussion that led up to the change of piano had taken their toll. I was quite upset, and I was convinced my emotion would leak through into my playing and be captured on the disc for ever, making people feel mysteriously low when they listened to it. However, when I received the finished product half a year later, there was no trace. The music sounded serene, and the reviewers said so too. That was a good thing. But I have also had the experience of feeling particularly moved when recording certain passages, and finding that nothing 'extra' has found its way on to the disc. That's not so good.

We've all seen famous performers who emote violently

when they play, 'performing' the emotions of the music as well as the music itself. We hear a lot these days about 'ownership of the material', but with artists like Jacqueline du Pré or Leonard Bernstein it almost seemed the other way round; they seemed 'possessed' by the music. Undoubtedly they felt it deeply, and fans loved their involvement, but for me this type of performance is counterproductive. I feel I'm being invited to witness them having an emotional experience, and this prevents me from having one myself. What such performers offer me is not the music but the spectacle of their own passion.

At the opposite extreme are undemonstrative players whose composure hides a selfless control of the instrument. They try scrupulously to bring the music to life without getting in the way. Obviously one can't help watching them, and sensing their physical presence, but their body language is carefully restrained in order not to draw attention to the messenger rather than the message. Think of Sviatoslav Richter sombrely reading his way through a piano recital by the dim light of an anglepoise lamp, or the startling virtuosity that poured out of Rachmaninov as he sat almost unmoving and poker-faced at the piano. The music lived through them, but they didn't have to mime its emotions to make it comprehensible.

There are some players who just feel deprived if they can't emote on stage, and others who feel guilty if they do. The audience's reaction is not something that can be second-guessed in either event, and as well as varying from person to person, can vary from one nationality to another. In one country they may love it if you throw yourself around. In another they may admire you more if you keep absolutely still. In Britain at the moment, the public seems to have a yearning to let its famously stiff upper lip wobble, and is more open to displays of emotion than it used to be. The less familiar the audience is with the music, the more they seem to like having it signposted by the performer's body language and expressions. If, on the other hand, musicians are playing to an audience of colleagues, they instinctively rein in their explanatory gestures.

You can't control how any gesture will be interpreted by your audience. When playing chamber music, I find I often feel like sharing certain nice moments in the music by looking over to a colleague, perhaps smiling, or gently drawing attention to a moment where a melody passes from me to them or vice versa. This would happen naturally in a rehearsal, and feels like an appropriate part of performing the music too. Recently, though, I found myself saying something of the kind to our host after a private concert. She said, 'Oh, do you do that deliberately? I noticed you turning to look at your colleagues, and I couldn't help being surprised that you still needed to do that after so many years of playing together.' For her, my gesture was not illuminating; in fact, she took it as evidence of insecurity. Perhaps it would have been more convincing if I never looked round at all, but for me this would have meant consciously restraining myself. As a listener I have just the opposite response to a player who never looks away from the music or from their hands; I feel they don't know the music well enough to be free.

Students often ask whether it's important to 'put yourself into' the music. My answer is that it isn't something you have to strive consciously to do. Other people can't help noticing how you look and move, and your presence – physical and spiritual – is an integral part of your performance. There may be value in learning to control distracting gestures and superfluous movement, but no player needs to strive to *put themselves in* to the music, because they are there anyway as the vessel through which the music passes. In any case, many performers spend too much effort on trying to project a certain image. It's an illusion to think that you can fully control how the audience sees you, and ultimately whether they like you or not depends on them, not you.

The player will certainly make an impact on the audience. Much less sure is whether the *music* will come across to them. In every field of music, fans have a special love for those performers who give us the music as the primary experience, and themselves as the secondary experience. Audiences sense where the performer's priorities lie, and for whose sake they are in the business of performance.

L is for Layout

In the middle of a concert tour recently I opened my suitcase in St Gallen in Switzerland to find that the score of the first work in the programme, a Haydn trio, was not there. I phoned the concert hall in Amsterdam where we had been the night before. Not there. It wasn't in the hotel either. Fortunately, there was a music shop in the town and even more fortunately, an hour before the concert, I was able to buy the very volume of trios I needed. It was in a different edition from the one from which I had learned the work and which I had used for every performance, but I was glad to have it.

Hardly having had a moment to look at it, I used the new edition in the concert. It was surprisingly disconcerting to have the music laid out in a different way from the copy that I was used to. It started on a right-hand page instead of the left. There was a different number of bars on each page, so all the page turns were in different places. I don't look at the music all that much in a performance, but at certain moments I glance at it to check this and that. During the performance I glimpsed in my usual way, only to find the wrong bar looking back at me. The effect was slightly dizzying. Bars that were previously on my right were now on my left and vice versa.

I became aware that my knowledge of the piece had incorporated a geographical image of the score. The opening theme *belonged* in the top-left corner of the page. During certain passages I expect the page-turner to stand up, and I'm used to seeing their arm cross my field of vision as I play particular notes. It was odd to have the page-turner keep quiet during those moments, but stand up during others. The slow movement usually ends at the bottom of a left-hand page, and I can proceed seamlessly to the finale without a page-turn or a noise – but not in the new copy.

Curiously, there were gains as well. Just because of the font used, or the surprising location of a certain passage on the page, the new edition made me aware of the beauty of certain phrases which I had grown used to. For some reason, in the crisp black printing of the new edition, they leaped out at me like a restored oil painting. Even something necessitating a turn of the head to the right instead of to the left made me see it afresh. Clever old Haydn!

Everyone who memorises music will know that the look of the music on the page is an important aid. Many players have a degree of photographic memory; when they know the music well, they actually 'turn the page' in their head as they play. The disposition of notes on the page becomes built in to their memorised version of the music. If this photographic image were to be erased, leaving only the sound of the music and the muscle memory of the fingers, many players would be seriously discomfited. The physical appearance of the score is not, you might think, part of the music itself, but it becomes inseparably linked to it for many performers. The same is, I suppose, true for actors who memorise their lines from a certain edition of the play. And it must also be so for dancers who learn a role on a certain stage and are accustomed to using details of the building to 'check' the degree of turn, the length of a leap, and so on. I can still 'see' the pages of many pieces of music I learned as a child, complete with their illustrations. Even when I hear, say, the Vienna Philharmonic playing the Blue Danube waltz on New Year's Day, I see the orange volume of the Children's Strauss from which I learned a simple version of it, and can superimpose the image of the score on what I hear them play.

Since losing my Haydn score, I've become more aware of the peripheral aspects of memory, which turn out to be not so peripheral after all. Driving a familiar route through rural England to another concert, I realised that the way the landscape opens out at a certain point in the journey is linked, for me, to the way it appears from inside the car. The beauty of the view lies partly in the way the land falls away on the right, revealing a horizon which on this particular route is only ever seen through the side windows, never through the front. I have incorporated the framing aspect of the car windows into my memory of this view, which always demands a turn of the head in a certain direction, a glance upwards, a private satisfaction that it only appears in my peripheral vision.

M is for Modulation

Turning the calendar over to a new month one morning, I found that the next picture was one of Hokusai's *Thirty-six views of Mount Fuji*. It shows labourers unloading stores from a barn while invisible hands control kites flying merrily in the air above it, and the mountain looks on serenely in the background. What a good idea this Japanese contemporary of Beethoven's had, to show Mount Fuji from lots of different perspectives, often as the backdrop to a busy scene of everyday life. The mountain looks different from each place. We are not shown an iconic view of Mount Fuji as visitors from all over the world would recognise it; travelling around it is the point. Yet we know that the mountain is the home key, so to speak, of the whole series.

I started to think about the idea of travelling away from an agreed reference point to look at it from different angles, or under different light conditions. The Impressionist painters, for example, have given us beautiful meditations on the same building or scene varying in colour at different times of day. But even more intriguing is the idea of going away to look at something familiar from several viewpoints. In music this has a parallel in the art of modulation, which plays such a crucial role in Western music from the seventeenth century onwards. All such pieces base their structure on the idea of starting out from a home key, travelling to a closely related key to present a new idea, roaming through a number of adventurously distant keys, and then returning to the home key where the original theme re-emerges. Listeners do not need to be able to identify the actual keys to sense that the music is moving to different regions, and they have a satisfying consciousness of a journey away from and back to a homeland.

In the development of Western classical music, the journeys undertaken from the home key got gradually bolder. In Bach's and Mozart's days there was generally a foray from the home key to what musicians call the 'dominant' key, or from the key of, say, C major to the key of G major. Other nearby keys, related by the laws of the harmonic series and how the ear hears, are the subdominant (F major if you start off in C major) and the relative minor (A minor in the key of C). Each had a distinct feeling associated with it and was used to create a sense of emotional contour within the piece. Then, moving further away from the home key, it was possible to use satellites of those related keys to journey even further away. But in large-scale works of the Classical period one never travels far away without returning. Knowing where you are and coming home at the end of the day is a structure taken for granted by those composers. It is, of course, a psychological need embedded in the heart of most listeners too.

The idea of key modulation, so central to European music, is unimportant in other cultures. Indian music, for example, has a structure more akin to Western variation form, or verse form. A melodic cell or motif introduced at the beginning, anchored to a drone bass, gathers complexity and activity as it is repeated many times. As a listener one's focus is on the organic growth from a simple shape to one densely packed with emotion and energy. Modulation in the Western sense is not one of its gambits. We remain conscious of the drone bass insisting on where we belong, the pulse that beats quietly in between the verses, and will be beating quietly when all the activity is over. From stillness to energy and back, or from simplicity to complexity, but not from home to a faraway place and back.

By contrast the great works of Western music from the Baroque onwards all explore the idea of a journey and a landscape. For several hundred years the journey was circular. Musical forms played on everyone's understanding that the home key was where you lived, but you were happy to be shown the next garden and even the top of the hill, from which you would glimpse distant prospects not imagined at first. This was a bit like a walk undertaken in a Jane Austen novel. However, to go off into those distant prospects and not come back . . . that was something not often undertaken until the late Romantic period and the early decades of the twentieth century, and even then it was psychologically daring. So many keys were used in a single piece that one lost a sense of how they related. The first key you heard might turn out not to be the home key at all, but merely the first in a series of exotic locations. You might start off somewhere and end up somewhere else entirely. And eventually the sense of where you were in the harmonic landscape became so loose that nobody knew what was home, what was away. You were in the musical equivalent of Jack Kerouac's *On the Road* or Paul Bowles's *The Sheltering Sky*, a journey where any and every place was of equal promise, where you might feel more at home in the desert than you did 'at home'. A new piece could no longer be pinned down as being 'in' a certain key, as one notices when reading concert programmes. Perhaps it will turn out that the development of modulation in music had a parallel in our changing attitudes to travel, and in the expanding possibilities of far-flung travel, especially as the twentieth century progressed.

But what is the point of travel? Is it to see somewhere new, or is it to see your familiar place from somewhere else? Is it more important to go away, or to come back? Which is more of a struggle, the leaving home or the returning? Is it necessary to forget your home when you are in another place, or should you always remember where you belong? Indeed, would you know you were travelling if you didn't know that you had a home? In classical pieces from Bach through Beethoven, Schubert and Brahms there is a reassuring convention that, however far away from the home key you modulate, there is a quick way back. At the end of the development section there is usually a brief, intense passage magically demonstrating in a few bars that you were closer to home than you thought. The journey away might have been arduous, but the return is as simple as opening a door and finding that you are back in your garden. The home territory had not let you go after all. And listen, here is the main theme again in its original key. Does it seem different because of where you have just been? Did you realise that Mount Fuji was always visible, even when you were flying your kite?

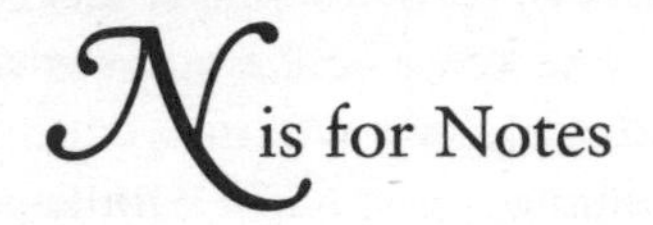

N is for Notes

If you were the first person who tried to devise a way of writing down music so that you could preserve it, what shape would you use for a sound?

Notes are single sounds in music, but they are also the name of the written version, the shapes that represent sounds in code. Notes have come to be linked inseparably with the shape we've long accepted as their scriptural counterpart: a round black head, usually with a tail or stem attached to it. Sing a note: la. Does it seem like a round, black object? Does it have a colour? Does it extend in space, like a line, a cone, a wave? As I sit here now, singing 'la', it seems to me that the sound might look like a child's drawing of a comet.

Whatever you might invent if you were to go back to the drawing-board on behalf of musicians, the prosaic fact is that we have come to think of notes as round black things on a white background. Indeed, musicians often refer to notes as 'the dots'. There must be musicians who don't read music and don't have this association with what a note is or looks like. But I have no idea whether 'note' carries a visual symbol for them, whether they simply hear the sound, or whether they have completely different flights of visual fancy.

Instruments that have keys or holes of fixed pitch are said to 'have notes'. The piano has notes, the organ has notes, the recorder and the oboe have notes, but for many instruments there is a more fluid sense of what could be played where and how. Nobody talks of the human voice as having notes, though clearly notes are created by it. Instruments where the player can slide between sounds, like violins and cellos, or trombones, are not said to 'have notes'. Having notes implies ready-made units that produce the same pitch every time they are struck, plucked, or blown. Nevertheless there is no difference in the notation used for fixed-pitch instruments as distinct from instruments where the pitches have to be created. Everyone uses the same round black dots.

Notes on their lined background are the two-dimensional grid through which musicians have to see three, four dimensions and maybe more. They try to understand what is represented by the notes, whose visual appearance on the page is often no clue to the effect the music will make when it becomes sound. I once attended a concert in which a late Beethoven string quartet was played. One particular passage had a deeply spiritual atmosphere and a dense, concentrated sound which was so fascinating that after the performance I sneaked up to the stage and looked at the parts, still on the music stands. And what struck me was how simple, almost empty, the music looked on the page. Conversely I have come across music that looks insanely complicated on the page, with rhythms of mind-boggling asymmetry, but the effect is unremarkable, even emotionally dull. I now realise that there is no predictable relationship between the complexity on the page and the complexity of the musical effect.

Bach made a remark about notes which is often taken out of context and quoted as a philosophical wisecrack.

Speaking about the organ, for which he wrote so many magnificent works, he said, 'There is nothing to it. You only have to play the right notes in the right order, and the instrument plays itself.' This was a remark about a semi-mechanical instrument whose tone, unlike that of most instruments, cannot be varied during the length of the note. But the saying is often quoted admiringly by players who think that Bach said, 'There is nothing to playing music. You only have to play the right notes in the right order.'

This, of course, is a completely different kettle of fish. I had often pondered the devastating nonchalance of Bach's alleged witticism before I ever discovered that he was referring to the organ, and by then I had spent some time thinking about what he meant. The idea that all you have to do is to play the right notes in the right order is undoubtedly true, or at least part of the truth. But I was puzzled by the omission of 'at the right time' or 'with the right feeling'. In his actual remark about the organ he might have added that one has to play the right notes in the right order *and* at the right time. But perhaps a great composer considers the right time and incorporates it in his choice of note values, so playing the notes in the right order would automatically produce the right time. As for the right feeling, perhaps Bach thought that the need for it was blindingly obvious, or perhaps he was one of those composers who disapprove of players bringing their own emotions to bear on something whose feeling is inherent in its notes. If he hadn't been well known as a serious and devout person, one might just have suspected his remark about the organ of being ironical in the same sense as violinist Itzhak Perlman – who once in my hearing replied to the question, 'Do tell us what your marvellous violin is!' with the dry put-down, 'It's just a little wooden job.'

Notes swim before the inner eyes of all musicians who read from printed music, and I dare say that when they play music in their heads the image of printed notes is never completely absent. In the early days of Western notation the notes were more like rhombuses or diamonds, and in many composers' manuscripts they look a bit like diagonal scratches. After all, note, from Latin *nota*, just means a mark. But rhombus, diamond and scrawl have long given way to round notes; empty round heads for longer notes, filled-in heads for shorter ones. The heads are shown on a system of five lines which locate the pitch. The stems have various kinds of hooks on their ends to show how long the note lasts. Head and stem together are like a little lollipop, or a little upright tadpole. There isn't much about it that looks musical, but it will have to do until somebody comes up with a new way of showing what a sound looks like. Contemporary composers have invented new graphics for their computer music, for example, but each person's system is more or less unique, and most publishers continue to rely on our rather limited conventional notation.

Notes are not the sounds, but symbols for them. For many people, there is more of a gap between printed notes and actual music than there is between printed words and their meaning. Indeed one could say that a written word *is* a word, but a written note is not a sound – only the representation of it, or the instruction for it. The distance between a printed score and a real musical performance is arguably a greater journey than from a printed play-script to a spoken play. There are skilled people (such as composers) who can sit down silently with a score, read it and 'hear' what the music would sound like if it were played. But lots of people, offered just the score, would hand it back saying, 'I can't hear that in my head. I need to hear it played.'

When you read text, you don't need to hear the words to understand them. Also, if the words are in the right order you will be able to extract meaning from them; how long each word lasts is not an indispensable part of the meaning. But in music, just to give the notes in the right order, without their durations, would destroy the meaning. I remember, as a child preparing for music theory exams, that I had to look up themes in a 'dictionary of musical themes' where well-known melodies were anatomised according to the letter-names of their notes. They were listed in the dictionary as a series of letters, all transposed into C major. 'Happy Birthday to You', for example, came out as GGAGCB and so on; the National Anthem as CCDBCD. Using this system, it was astonishing how themes that were wildly different from one another in their musical contexts looked almost identical. The other part of the dictionary listed those same themes in their musical notation, and when the rhythms and pitches were restored they all leaped back into their distinct characters, not similar at all.

For a long time there has been no other way but notes for a composer to communicate with musicians who live in a different place and maybe a different time. The most sweeping music, the most heart-rending phrases – for the purpose of writing them down, and for the purpose of learning them – have to be coldly divisible into little round black notes. 'What are days for? / Days are where we live . . . They are to be happy in: / Where can we live but days?' asks Philip Larkin.* And for musicians it is the same with notes.

* 'Days', from *The Whitsun Weddings* (Faber, 1964)

O is for Old

It's long been my habit, before concerts begin, to stand in the wings or behind the stage curtain and look at the audience or listen to the sound of their chatter. This may sound secretive, but it helps me to get into the right mood for the concert. On concert days there is often a long and numbing journey to reach the hall. Of course I try to shake off the feeling of lethargy that often settles on me during a journey, but it isn't always easily shaken off. Changing into concert clothes is usually some kind of mood enhancer, but even better is to stand near the audience and sense the buzz that usually permeates the hall. Their pleasant anticipation awakens me to a sense of occasion, even if I didn't feel it moments before.

While peeping from behind the curtain or the stage door, I often see just a vertical slice of the audience right through the hall from the cheap seats to the expensive ones, and what I see is a cascade of silver heads. Our audiences are not only mature, but of mature years. The funny thing is that I have been seeing exactly this silver cross-section ever since I played my first professional concerts a quarter of a century ago. I was young then, and I am catching up with them in age, but my visual impression of our audiences has been remarkably consistent. My colleagues and I used to comment on the age gap between us and our audiences, wondering where our fellow young people were. We wondered what it said about us that we had chosen to devote ourselves to music which seemed to appeal to an older crowd. Were we prematurely old?

As time went by we found opportunities to ask members of the audiences about their concert-going habits. Many people told us that they had only come to appreciate classical music, and in particular chamber music, as they grew older. They said it didn't attract them when they were younger, but as time went by they discovered that other sorts of music, which previously held their attention, had lost their charm. Conversely, the sort of music we play, which used to mean little to them, had come to seem emotionally rewarding. They wondered how they had managed to ignore it for so long.

We could not precisely compare our experience to theirs because they were listeners, and we were participants. It's much easier to see the virtues of an art-form if you are inside it, making it happen, getting the direct benefit; the satisfaction of playing chamber music to a high level can be independent of having an audience. In our teenage years (and sometimes before) we had all been led into chamber music as a participant sport. Our interest in it was as players, not as customers. We could never say whether we'd have found our own way into ticket-buying audiences if we had experienced chamber music solely as listeners. It puzzled us that they had taken so long to find us, but we enjoyed their thoughtful concentration once they had.

'Old' is a word I have heard constantly in my working life. The music itself is usually old, the way of playing is linked to old styles of playing, the instruments are old, the audiences are old. 'Why do you keep on playing old music?' ask young friends who don't yet realise where some of their pop heroes got their musical ideas. Yet for me and my colleagues, music from several centuries ago is not a worn-out concept, but an imaginative link between us and like-minded people who are no longer physically around. Among people who talk about the 'authentic performance' of old music, it is now generally accepted that one cannot really know how people used to play, or how they heard and interpreted their music. But to be actively engaged with old music is the nearest thing I know to travelling in a time-machine. I would not claim to know how (for example) Schubert played or what he wanted his interpreters to do, but I would certainly say that playing his music keeps his thoughts and feelings alive in a way that makes it almost irrelevant that he himself has gone. By playing his music we evoke its expressive power right now, in the twenty-first century. But the time-travelling feels as if it works both ways: we can usher him into the present, but we can also usher ourselves into the past. I don't claim, of course, that we emerge with any knowledge of the circumstances of the 1820s or anything like that. I simply mean that all musicians know that music of long ago is not threadbare or obsolete if it is brought to life sympathetically by players of today. 'Old' has no pejorative meaning for us, almost the reverse. In some ways I think we all see ourselves – musicians from different centuries – as strung out across the timeline, separated in a random kind of way that becomes meaningless once we make imaginative contact. The fact that some of us are 'in the past' and others 'in the future' seems irrelevant. I would go so far as to say that although rationally I understand that a favourite composer such as Schumann, who died in 1856, is no longer with us, he has been as present in my working life as most of my actual companions, and has made as much impact. In the subjective sphere of my musical life I regard him neither as dead nor as old.

I read a newspaper article recently about the warehouse fire in 2004 which destroyed numerous works of modern British art, including many pieces by controversial young BritArt stars such as Tracey Emin and Jake and Dinos Chapman. Many paintings and works of the generation before theirs were also destroyed in the fire. Asked whether they felt sad that the works of that older generation had vanished, the young BritArtists said that it was not a significant loss for them because they had not been influenced by the older artists in any case. The writer commented that many artists like to claim that they were not influenced by their parents' generation, but these young artists really meant it. They felt they were working in a new way, expressing themselves with ideas and materials of a different kind, not dependent on their elders for inspiration. They clearly prided themselves on having escaped the old. Perhaps they deceive themselves in thinking that their work is new, but they were clearly determined to be seen as having broken the link with their teachers' generation.

Cutting yourself off from previous generations is something alien to most musicians in whatever field they work. New instruments evolve from time to time, but we still work with sound, the same material we have always worked with, the same material that all musicians work with. We can't tell the world that we have now abandoned that old material, paint, or that old material, stone, and have moved on to express ourselves in sharks and unmade beds. Despite John Cage, we musicians are still working with sound waves and the predisposition of the human ear to assess harmony and discord in ways that, despite all experimentation and shock tactics, remain fundamentally unchanging. There are probably more new ways of seeing than there are of hearing.

Music has no 'material' that can go in and out of fashion. We still make sounds that unfold in time and draw the listener's attention along with them, just as we always did. We feel part of a continuum of music and musicians. I have no sense, when I play, that I am doing anything new. This is not to say that I don't have my own thoughts about the music, thoughts that make me play in a slightly different way from everybody else, and which make my style recognisable. But I don't regard newness as a particularly important aspect of my work, or a particularly meaningful one. It may be, indeed, that my most satisfying moments are when I have delved deep enough into something to make its oldness disappear. And the feeling of oldness disappearing is perhaps something our mature audiences, too, enjoy at our concerts.

P is for Playing Along

If you are a soloist preparing to play a concerto, how do you practise playing with the orchestra? All your practice is done at home without an orchestra, and you will have perhaps just one rehearsal with them, probably on the day of the concert. In the mean time, how do you prepare for the experience of hearing a big orchestra round about you, listening to them and counting silent bars in all the places where the soloist doesn't play?

If you play anything other than a piano, you can ask a pianist to play the orchestral part with you. But if you are a pianist, you can't do that unless you have access to a room with two pianos in it, and not many people do. Never having had two pianos in my home, I have followed since childhood the dubious habit of playing along with other people's recordings so that I get used to the entrances and exits of the orchestra. I'm not talking about copying another pianist's approach to the music, of course; that is a very bad idea. I'm talking simply about getting used to all the places in which the soloist has to dovetail with the orchestra during a concerto.

First of all, I have to have the good luck to find a recording which is compatible with the pitch of my piano. If the recording was made many years ago (when pitch was a touch lower) or more recently in America or mainland

Europe (where it is likely to be higher) there will be a painful conflict between the pitch of the recording and of my piano. When I was a child, playing along with an LP recording, my dad was prevailed upon to sit by the record player pressing lightly on the disc to slow it down and lower it from European pitch to ours. The finest calibration of touch was required to bring it exactly into line with my piano, but I seem to remember I complained ungratefully whenever his hand wavered, and the pitch with it. These days, with a CD, it is not possible to intervene in the same way, so if the pitch is wrong one is stuck with it.

Playing along with other pianists' recordings is a fascinating exercise, one I didn't realise was so difficult until I started doing it. You think you and the other pianist have both learned the same music, and if you agree on the basic tempo there should be no problem in keeping together. However, just a few bars will show that there are myriad inflections of time that make one person's playing different from another's. I start off playing exactly at the speed that so-and-so does, but by the end of the phrase we are apart. Neither of us may be intentionally bending the time to our expressive purposes. Yet we can't help doing it. One pianist's idea of how much direction and how much forward motion is needed – even if they think this is not a personal judgement but one that is suggested purely by the music – will be minutely different from another's. In the course of listening to someone's recording I can often 'learn' their sense of timing and reproduce it so that we stay together. This gives me a glimpse of what it must feel like to be them, to have their hands. Indeed copying another pianist's timing sometimes gives an eerie sensation of being them, making their decisions. For timing is probably the most crucially personal factor in a person's playing.

Not long ago I came back from the local library with a whole selection of recordings of the same concerto, Beethoven's Fourth, which I wanted to practise. All were more or less compatible in pitch with my own piano, so I was able to play along with them all. Yet I found that I could naturally keep pace with certain pianists and not at all with others. Some seemed to share my instinctive feeling for rubato and drive; in the background I could hear their playing more or less overlaying mine. But with others it was as though they were dealing with an entirely different material. They stretched, they languished, they plodded instead of flying. Or so it seemed to me; if the pianist on the record had been in the room, he or she would probably have said I was rushing. Intriguingly, I found that I was much more easily able to play along with recordings that are now 'historical', that is, half a century old. You might imagine that these old recordings were ponderous and cautious, but on the contrary, the older pianists such as Cortot, Rachmaninov and Schnabel seemed particularly fluent and mercurial. It was the more 'modern' recordings that seemed plodding.

I was once hired by a film studio to record some virtuosic Chopin that was being used for the soundtrack of the film *Persuasion*. The trouble was, they had already shot the film and edited it minutely to a certain pianist's recording which subsequently they could not get permission to use. They decided to hire me to play the same music. But because the film had already been edited to the split second using the original recording, they had to ask me to duplicate the other pianist's timing exactly. I had a copy of the scene in question and the original recording. I studied it and the frames of the film as best I could at home. The sailor's hat was thrown into the air at exactly such-and-such a moment, the horse neighed at another, the carriage door was flung open as a certain chord played.

I went into the studio and tried to duplicate what I had studied, leaving aside the original pianist's recording. But it proved almost impossible, tear-jerkingly so. Never before had I realised at this level of detail how obstinate is one's own sense of timing. The flustered producer kept telling me that I was one second too early on the shot of the horizon, two seconds late on the crow's nest, that the shot of the door closing was half a second out now with the end of the phrase. I tried and tried, but the next time there was a whole new sequence of incompatibilities. I thought I had digested the other pianist's way of doing things, but it remained elusive. My own sense of timing was not to be annihilated. My recording was used on the film, but they had to tweak it after I had gone. And in the end it was quite a good feeling that I was unable to stop being me.

Q is for Quiet

When I wondered aloud what topic was best for the letter Q, my daughter immediately said, 'You should call it "Q is for Quiet" – you use that word such a lot!'

This surprised me, because I worry that I spend a lot of the day making a noise, or at least making sounds that might disturb other people. I've always been very aware that my practising and rehearsing, while simply representing work – sorry, beautiful music – to me, is quite possibly a nuisance to someone else. Even music-lovers in the house find it difficult at times, such as when they are trying to do homework. So I said, 'Are you sure I use the word "quiet" a lot?' 'You use it all the time!' said my family. 'You're always complaining about noise from outside, noise from neighbours, noise from other people's music, and you're always saying you need to "go and be quiet".'

When I think about it, it is true that I have always favoured quiet, not only as a contrast to noise, but as a sound level. As a child I always liked quiet music and, given the choice, would pick a quiet piece rather than a loud piece to play in concerts or competitions. I found this was unusual in my peer group, which generally preferred loud and fast music. I enjoy a blast of loud music with the best of them, but unlike some of my contemporaries I didn't feel that loudness should be the prevailing mode. Quiet music for me was not simply loud music with the volume turned down. It seemed to me (and it still does) that what quiet music said was truer and more worth hearing than what loud music said. But it was often put to me by adults that by selecting a quiet piece for a competition, I was throwing away my chances of winning a prize. Fortunately that didn't turn out to be true, though adjudicators often commented that it was daring of me to stake my chances on a quiet piece. I confess I doubted my own ability to bring off a barnstorming piece of loudness and speed, but that wasn't the main reason for my choice, which reflected a preference for quieter music. Even today I notice that I choose to listen to CDs at a lower level than many other people do. I'm the one who always seems to be turning the radio down. So perhaps there is some physiological imperative, though whether of ears or nerves I couldn't say.

A career in music is obviously concerned with sound and performance in myriad ways. One is conscious of oneself as a person whose work is noisy – pleasantly noisy, one hopes, but still an interruption of calm. As my musical life has become more and more time-consuming, so, proportionately, a need for quietness has grown. While I enjoy the hours spent making music, there is a definite cut-off point beyond which it seems to produce a fatigue of my ears and nervous system. When I am practising the piano alone at home, I stop every little while, go out of the room and do something else for a few minutes to give my ears and my concentration some recovery time. At the end of a long rehearsal, I dislike going into another room to find that the radio is on. I don't even like finding that a lively conversation is in progress, especially if I'm expected to join in. I need the sound to stop for a while. It seems that my conscious adoption of a life of public sound and noise has caused a counterthrust of equal magnitude in the opposite direction. I may actively need music, but I actively need quiet as well. I need to go away and digest what has been said, thought and expressed. I can't possibly do this if I myself am continuously required to express things, whether in words or music.

On concert days, especially, I feel strongly that I need some quiet time between rehearsal and concert. I certainly don't join my colleagues in practising and playing right up to the moment that the concert begins. Admittedly this is partly because there is often no piano in the backstage room. But even when there is, I quite often leave the lid closed over the keyboard unless some technical problem, such as a tricky fingering that slipped out of my grasp in the rehearsal, is nagging at me. I feel that if there is a continuum of sound running right up to the concert, the performance will not feel in any way special. Yes, the intensity of our playing might increase on stage, and the atmosphere in the hall will add its own excitement, but I find that the concert is much more welcome if it emerges from a background of quiet. Music being played close to me claims my attention. I have to listen, and I have to hear. It's as though my ears get supersaturated and when that happens, my concentration is reduced. It's for this reason that I often leave the dressing room, where my colleagues are practising, and go and hang around close to the stage, where I can hear the quietness of the hall. This somehow provides a sense of the calm background on to which our performance will be imprinted.

At various times I have taken part in workshops designed to tackle performance nerves, to enhance the performer's enjoyment of the 'concert situation', or simply to explore what it is that goes on in the performer's mind. This has made me aware that the art of performance is (or should be) the art of giving. No musician I know has become thoroughly immune to the strangeness of being on stage, facing hundreds of people avid for a good experience. Every one of us feels the pressure, sometimes in the form of excitement, sometimes in the form of fear, not infrequently in the form of a strong disinclination to put oneself through this particular mill again. Some players consciously cut themselves off from the audience and imagine that they are playing to satisfy themselves alone. However, there usually comes a shocking moment when they glance up from their shell and realise that they are surrounded by hundreds of people paying close attention. The players most adapted to concert performance actively embrace the fact that the hall is full of listeners. They consciously reach out and include the audience in their awareness. They look right to the back of the hall, and up to the galleries, and they try to imagine being out there looking back. Their performance is consciously broadcast to the whole room, and the audience feels it.

This conscious inclusion of the audience is effective and necessary for many performers, but it is mentally and emotionally taxing. For me it is, in fact, the equivalent of walking on stage, taking a deep breath and exhaling for two hours without stopping. This feeling of large-scale exhalation is bound up with the effort of producing sound and performing music. When the concert is over, I have an overwhelming need to counterbalance the whole experience by inhaling. To say this is not only a metaphor, for I often come offstage actually feeling that my breathing has been peculiar, and that I need to sit down somewhere and breathe normally. Exhaling – sending the music out into the hall on a wave of concentration – has come to be almost synonymous with producing sound and 'giving' to the audience. It's hardly surprising that I can only breathe in again by immersing myself in quietness. Sharing music with the audience can be very satisfying, but I have come to realise that for me, at least, quietness is literally the inspiration.

R is for Rehearsal and Repetition

In order to economise on rehearsal time and performance anxiety, my trio has been trying to organise more logical sequences of works that we offer to concert organisers. If we don't keep an eye on it, we find ourselves with a different programme for each concert – particularly these days, when many concert organisers like to plan series around 'themes' that mean that our programme has to be tailored to them alone. If we allow each promoter to request a different programme, we have to find time for separate rehearsals for each one, and it's extremely labour-intensive. If, on the other hand, we manage to create a 'run' of performances of the same pieces, we are faced with the problem of repetition: how to stop things becoming stale.

Rehearsal and repetition. Curiously, these are the English and French words, respectively, for the same thing. What we call a rehearsal is 'une répétition' in France; I always thought it a poor description of a process that accounts for at least half of a musician's working life. I'm making a distinction here between private practice, which takes place alone, and rehearsal, which is a collective process undertaken by a group of players. For all of us, the time spent giving concerts is only the tip of the iceberg. Rehearsal occupies far more time and often more energy, partly because it thrusts the players into a minefield of diplomatic niceties. Firstly, it is often difficult to put into words one's sense of what the music means or how to make it expressive. In any group, there are always people better at it than others, or just quicker to find a form of words. This can drive others further into their shells, or force them to agree to something just because they haven't yet figured out a way of countering it. Equally, if they are sensitive, articulate people get frustrated if they have to bite their tongues in order to give others time to formulate their views. Everyone constantly asks themselves whether pressing for a certain result will bring out the best from the others, or do the opposite. Even with a seasoned group, people can be amazingly touchy.

Alas, it is often true that musicians don't know what to do in rehearsal except to repeat things. The kind of questions they ask themselves privately, while practising, are put on the back-burner when they join the group. When I give coaching sessions to chamber groups I find that, nine times out of ten, they don't know why they are playing things in the way that they are; if they are able to keep together they assume that their way is successful. No one (except perhaps the conductor of an orchestra) likes to assume responsibility for questioning or directing the playing of the whole group, so they fall back on playing things through, having a breather and then playing them through again. Actually, some problems do naturally disappear during a process of *repetition*, while others will never be tackled.

By contrast, I always thought rather smugly that the English word 'rehearsal' was a superior term. For many years, in fact, I thought that rehearsal implied a process of *re-hearing*. That was a pleasant metaphor for what goes on in such sessions – hearing things in a new way, taking other people's opinions on board, adding new perspectives, going forward with them. However, a foreign visitor to my house once told me that she had never come across the English word 'rehearsal' before, and what did it actually mean? I started to explain that it described our practice sessions and meant 'hearing again', but felt a twinge of doubt and went to look it up.

It turned out to come from the old French 're-hercer' and a *herce* is a harrow, so 'rehercer' is a process of ploughing up and turning over. This was even better than my notion of re-hearing, and comes much closer to my actual experience of rehearsing. For a lot of rehearsal is concerned with hearing criticism and suggestions from others, as well as giving such criticism oneself. This is something not many workers have to confront on a daily basis, but musicians mutually (though with some chagrin) accept it as the quickest way to achieve deep penetration of the music. We all know that the process of ploughing takes place so that seeds may be sown and subsequently grow. So if I say that rehearsal is a harrowing experience, I have the double sense of a phrase both etymologically and emotionally true.

I confess that sometimes, when time is short and people are tired after travelling, rehearsal does indeed become repetition. This has its place as well. We just need to check that we all remember (or still agree on) the precise speeds for different movements, the way we've planned to get from one section to another, the alignment of technically difficult moments. It does also happen, however, that what was supposed to be merely a check turns out to be rehearsal after all. Although time may be short, one or more players will suddenly declare that they are unhappy with the way we have been playing something, or more alarmingly, that we have lost sight of its meaning or motivation. In my group, such a feeling usually strikes only one person (always a different one) but it's accepted that we mustn't brush it off. How a player hangs on to their sense of meaning is very personal and constantly shifting. But if it slips, we all have to be willing at least to 're-hear' if not to plough things up and create space for the seeds of some new ideas.

Words for rehearsal are intriguing in other languages too. In German it is 'Probe', and in Italian, 'prova' – both meaning 'to try', to test or prove. For me these have pleasant echoes of the stage in bread-making known as 'proving' the dough, where the yeast takes effect and the dough begins to rise. The image sums up what happens during a good rehearsal. Rather sweetly, a friend of mine used to have a phrase for what we did when we'd finished rehearsing. 'Let's bake through the movement now,' she would say. We used the phrase for ages afterwards because it was a nice reference to what happens at the end of a batch of work. But people who bypass the rehearsal process and go straight from sightreading to concerts are likely to produce performances that are half-baked.

S is for Shifting Insights

When I was a child I used to put pencil marks in the margins of books to denote passages I thought especially interesting or wise. I wanted to be able to refer to them again, but when I did so, sometimes years later, they seemed less relevant than they once did. For now a different set of passages jumped out of the text at me. I sometimes even rubbed out the original marks, which seemed to reflect badly on my younger self. It could be the other way round: I was impressed by my earlier perspicacity. Some passages had kept their force, while others made me think, 'Good Lord! How shallow I was to mark that, not the other, a page later, which is so much wiser!'

I came to think of good books as a repository of insights waiting to be plucked out by the right person at the right moment. More than that, they seemed to be a mirror of oneself at different times. I knew that if I picked them up again in ten years' time, very likely a whole different set of things would seem poignant, helpful or true. I now rather wish I'd dated my pencillings, which could have amounted to an archaeology of my thoughts at different times.

Scholars say that a writer can never know how the book will be read. The author has to release the text to fly on its own, unable to control what it will mean to any given reader. Recently, a BBC Radio 4 programme asked women to nominate the book they felt had most influenced their lives. I heard a selection of their nominations, and was struck by the fact that everyone chose books they just happened to read while something emotional or difficult was going on in their lives. The book they nominated had helped them to escape, to forget, or had shone a helpful light on their situation. Nobody had picked a book read in neutral peacetime, as it were, a book that transcended personal circumstances and gave them insights they could apply to different situations. But perhaps any good book, containing a range of compelling observations, would have seemed magically relevant to a person with heightened sensitivity. I'd guess that, for example, George Eliot's *Middlemarch* or Tolstoy's *War and Peace* would always supply something exactly right for anyone in reflective mood.

When musicians rehearse things, we imagine we are taking our cues from the piece itself. We try to find what's important and let it shine through. But just as with books and readers, there is always a two-way process we're not really aware of. Somehow, in order to devote myself to the work of interpretation, I think of the music as active, and myself as neutral – or myself as empty, and the music as full – though the reality is much more complex.

I and my colleagues spend a lot of time in rehearsal talking about what the music 'needs'. It may seem crowded and cluttered, and calls for us to pick out what really matters. It may seem that a certain piece has been played too quickly and casually, that now we need to calm it down and make it clear. Or it may seem that someone else's part is more important than you had thought before. Perhaps it seems that a sense of drama is lacking, or conversely, that our playing is too dramatic and needs to be contemplative instead. In all these cases, we profoundly believe that we have received this message from the music itself. We feel another layer of the composer's thinking has revealed itself to us, or that we have discovered it. Either way, the source of inspiration is the piece of music. It is like a diamond with internal fire; held and twirled this way and that, it glows in different facets.

We often remark that when we return to a piece of music after a rest, it seems mysteriously to have changed, often to have matured. It seems to have been growing while we were away, and now presents us with new aspects of wisdom. We think how clever the composer is, and how much he has put into the piece. Sometimes he even seems to have sunk a delayed depth-charge in the music which goes off years after you first got to know it. But perhaps this attributes too much power to the score, and not enough to the musician. If a piece appears deeper and more sensitive than it did before, it's not because the music has changed, but because the musician has.

I was recently asked to play a Mozart piano quartet which I used to perform regularly with very good colleagues over a period of at least a decade. We had rehearsed and discussed it endlessly, trying (so I thought) every plausible approach in the course of the years. After the group disbanded, I didn't play the piece for a long time. I didn't think about it, nor did I hear it performed by anyone else. But when I picked it up again, I immediately and effortlessly saw new ways of playing all kinds of things, ways that had never occurred to me in all those rehearsals and performances. I used to think that achieving clarity was the minimum task of interpretation. But now it seemed to me that this same clarity was merciless. I saw – or at any rate, it now struck me – that some consoling shadows might be welcome. My view of the piece hadn't changed, but perhaps my understanding of context had.

Non-musicians may think it obvious that musicians bring their own insights to the music. But we think we're looking for timeless truths *in the music*. As a bonus, we may accept that there are layers of truth supplied by us according to each person's psychological state, but progress along psychological lines is bumpy and erratic. Nobody can guarantee being wiser next time we sit down to work on something. In the meantime, we think of the music as having the power to animate us, for it is the constant thing in a world of shifting and unreliable identities. It seems to be the thing outside ourselves, the thing on which we can work. But in truth it is not outside, and nor perhaps is it the thing on which we work.

Fresh from some argument at home, we come to the rehearsal with antennae bristling, and find drama and tension in the music. Fresh from a happy activity, we find new moments of resolution in the music. Sympathetic to a colleague because they've just said or done something sweet, we may find their part in the music unexpectedly enjoyable. I thought about all this recently when, in several consecutive rehearsals, a colleague commented that we were always 'letting the tempo fall forward' and that we should take more care to keep things stable and strict. The rest of us didn't feel we were falling forward, but tried to act on his comments, and in fact we did seem to find some new stability, a new attitude which gave us room to breathe. Some days later, over dinner, this same person – talking about his private life – said that he felt everybody was pushing him to 'move on', and that he was digging his heels in because he didn't feel ready. He said he wanted to go at a very steady pace until he could see where the right move was. I realised that he had been saying exactly the same things in rehearsals, but they were presented as purely musical comments, evoked precisely by the piece we were working on.

At that moment, I suddenly saw that the engine of insight was the player, not the music. More: the engine was the drama in which the player was currently engaged. Suddenly I wondered which is passive and which is active – the player or the music? Who energises which, or which whom? Insights seem to flash from one to the other like sparks of electricity, shuttling back and forth, lighting up sometimes the musician and sometimes the music. When we sit down to rehearse, we think we are setting aside our personal lives and putting ourselves at the service of the music, emptying ourselves so that it can fill us. But whether we know it or not, the way we play and the things we choose to bring out, or ignore, are a chart of our current state. As we attempt to bring the piece to life, our performance is an unwitting description of us. We are lit up as we try to illuminate.

T is for Talking to the Audience

The house lights go down. The musicians come on to the stage. Applause, followed by silence. The music begins. For some people, this is a moment of magical transition to a world in which music sheds light on our emotional lives. But others are intimidated by it. Why? The formal dress, the silence, perhaps insecurity in the face of an art-form that can be daunting and complex? For various such reasons, classical musicians these days are being encouraged to talk to their audiences, and put them at their ease, more than they used to.

Recently a conductor friend was preparing to perform Beethoven's 'Eroica' symphony. That season with his orchestra he had started talking to the audience, telling them a little historical background about the piece they were about to hear. This is not something that conductors have routinely been expected to do, and he had devoted some time to thinking how best to do it. On this occasion, however, he suddenly felt he wanted to focus entirely on the music. So he told the orchestra during the interval that he was planning not to speak, but just to launch into the symphony without preamble. The orchestra was aghast. 'Are you kidding? You have to speak. Everyone loves it when you speak – it makes them think that you are a human being.'

He agreed to introduce the symphony and made a very good job of it. In the bar afterwards, I was chatting to members of the audience, and sure enough, someone said to me, 'I'm not a regular concert-goer, and what particularly impressed me was that the conductor actually spoke to us before the symphony. It made me realise that he was a human being.'

This kind of remark has been made to me so many times that I accept the sincerity of it. I am all in favour of introducing pieces to audiences and have been doing it for years. However, it still bewilders me that our playing doesn't make it abundantly obvious that we're human. Why is a spoken introduction important? Musicians play their hearts out, giving the fruits of long thought and study, displaying a range of emotions and skills that are rarely encountered in everyday life, but listeners still seem thirsty for some additional kind of bridge between player and audience.

When my former group Domus started introducing pieces to the audience, it was part of a philosophy of sharing as much as possible about the musical experience. Talking to the audience, however, proved to be an ordeal for all of us, no matter how much we approved the principle. We found that, even if we were calm before the performance, speaking to the audience made our hearts pound and our limbs shake. We would sit down to play with trembling hands that were difficult to control. How curious that speaking should have this effect on us, when we were quite happy to play something extremely difficult in public without being unduly nervous! We persisted because we could see that people liked hearing us speak, but to be honest it was often a relief when it was someone else's turn. It felt as if speaking required a different part of the brain to jump into action.

An actor would find it hard to come on stage at the start of the evening, talk about what it's like to play Hamlet, and then walk off stage and come back as Hamlet. And I have no doubt that a dancer would find it difficult to walk to the footlights and verbalise to the audience about *Swan Lake* before taking up their opening pose in the ballet. In just the same way, we found it unsettling to introduce favourite pieces of music 'as ourselves' and then, without even leaving the stage, sit down and become part of the composer's vision. The 'I' who spoke and the 'I' who played didn't feel quite continuous, yet the act of speaking before playing made it seem that they were.

In more formal concert settings, the authorities sometimes actively discouraged us from speaking to the audience. It was viewed as non-serious, perhaps unwelcome because it shattered the reverent silence that falls between player and listener. But we spoke wherever we were allowed, and many people in the audience liked it. In fact, it was sometimes almost galling to be told what a difference one's speaking had made. Often I spoke for a couple of minutes, played for an hour, and then had people coming up to me to say how much they had appreciated my speaking. Well, you might conclude from that that my playing hadn't been any good, but I think it was more that the listeners were grateful to be addressed in words. Many people don't trust themselves to analyse a musical performance, but they know how to listen to the spoken word. Moreover, the spoken word made the player's personality instantly apparent. I always tried to think of something interesting to say, but I gradually realised that just hearing the player's voice was at least as important. The voice alone was enough to throw a filament between stage and stalls. Anyone who's been to a concert where the players remain silent until one of them is forced to introduce an encore will know the frisson of excitement which runs through the audience at hearing the voice. He's American! She has a deep voice! Funny use of English! Immediately they like us more.

Once on a concert tour we were playing a new piece by Judith Weir. We experimented with the performances, sometimes launching in without saying a word, sometimes introducing it and at shorter or greater length. It was obvious to all of us, rather annoyingly, that the more we said about it, the better the audience's response to the music. Where we said nothing at all, the reaction was muted, no matter how good the playing. Where we described our friendship with Judith, how she came to write the piece, what fun we had had rehearsing it and so on, the applause was noticeably warmer at the end.

As far as I know, musicians in past centuries have not had to speak about their music to get audiences on their side. Maybe this is partly because in earlier periods of music, performance often took place in front of an aristocratic audience in whose presence it would not have been appropriate to explain things. Performances in church would not have been suitable settings either. However, there were many famous musicians in the past hundred years – Rachmaninov, Kreisler, Paderewski, Heifetz – who made glittering careers without ever saying a word on stage except to introduce their encores. Nobody thought they weren't human as a result. Listeners accepted that they needed to gather their forces to play. The emotions expressed through their playing seemed to be enough to earn them devotion. Speaking on stage might even have dimmed their glamour.

Perhaps our current thirst for the human voice has been created by television and radio. We are so used to being talked at, bombarded with information, never left in silence for a moment, that it has become unthinkable for a performer to need and use silence. Nobody ever plays on TV without first being talked about, or talked to, or talking themselves. The space between us and the performer always has to be filled. Even the most specialist classical-music radio stations have announcers who talk right up to the moment the performance begins, and jump in as soon as it finishes in case we are discomfited by silence. Classic FM, one of the most successful radio stations, has found an enormous audience for classical music but it breaks the music into bite-sized chunks, keeping up a soothing commentary between numbers and constantly reassuring us that this is music to relax to, to help us chill out, to provide a pleasant working atmosphere. The aim is to make music slip easily down the throat, even if it happens to be a portrait of the composer's anguish.

Strangely, today music seems to need mediation, between player and listener, more than other art-forms. People go to art galleries and make their own minds up about silent works of art, however bizarre. They enjoy the toughest theatre pieces without anyone telling them what they're going to be about or what to think. They go into bookshops and pick up all manner of challenging books, plunging happily in without any helpful hints from the author. Nobody expects actors or dancers to chat to them at the start of a performance. Yet if people go to a concert where the music is played without comment, they seem to panic. The sight of performers preparing with silent concentration makes them uneasy. Because we often encounter music against a wall of chatter, it has become difficult for musicians to use silence without being threatening.

A hundred or two hundred years ago, people lived with silence much more than they do now. The silence that fell as an audience waited for a performer to play was no remarkable thing. Now, however, silence is a much rarer commodity, and can almost be intimidating. In the theatre we wait happily in the darkened hush before the curtain goes up, but in the concert hall people seem to hope for someone to come and relieve them of the silence. Television has trained us to think that we need a 'personality' to guide us into the entertainment, and that can only be done by talking. I can't think what Beethoven would say if he heard that his 'Eroica' symphony couldn't connect on a human level with the audience unless somebody spoke before it, but I imagine his response might not be in words at all.

U is for Unhelpful Thoughts

During a recent rehearsal for the Beethoven Triple Concerto for violin, cello and piano, my colleagues and I started talking about the thoughts that go through our heads during the long opening tutti played by the orchestra before the first entry of the three soloists. This opening section is a feature of most Classical concertos, and every soloist must have his or her own way of bridging those nerve-racking, adrenalin-filled minutes as they wait silently under the spotlight. Each member of my trio has experience of appearing as a concerto soloist. Moreover, we are used to spotlights, to large audiences, to taxing concert programmes. But we never exchanged our feelings about the particular case of the opening tutti (doesn't that sound like a Sherlock Holmes mystery?) until we were preparing the Triple Concerto for the umpteenth performance. 'Does anyone else have to fight off strange thoughts here?' one of us ventured. 'Yes!' chorused the others with relief.

I had privately wondered whether the thoughts that go through my head during the orchestral tutti were uniquely unhelpful, but it turned out that we all suffer from them. We agreed that those first minutes, the whole audience gazing at you as the orchestra surges around you, are some of the strangest in our musical lives. Though he wasn't writing about concertos, the poet Horace had a phrase which sums up our fears: 'The mountains go into labour, and there will be born an absurd little mouse.' You try not to fall victim to this psychological effect as the mountains labour around you. No, you will not be a ridiculous mouse. This time the mountains must give birth to a creature of legendary beauty.

The soloist is, so to speak, the eye of the storm. Most composers of concertos grasp at the chance to set up a dramatic dissonance between the huge noisy orchestra and the brave, lonely voice of the single instrument. As the orchestral introduction progresses, you feel the audience's concentration being gradually drawn from wide-angle down to pinpoint focus: from the big, sprawling orchestra to . . . you. All the sound and fury will be refined down to a moment where one person's line is offered as the antidote.

No matter how much preparation one has done for such a concert, it is very difficult not to wrestle with negative thoughts as you await your first entry. You find that you're not the unified person you thought you were; a malicious inner voice whispers that you're about to be horribly exposed. Often the worries concern memorisation. If you are playing from memory, you may suddenly be assailed by the thought that you have no idea what you are supposed to play when it is your turn. I have never forgotten the account given by a Scottish piano teacher who regaled some of us students with a description of his one and only appearance as a concerto soloist with a Glasgow orchestra. 'I was listening to the opening bars, and I suddenly realised I hadn't the slightest idea what I was supposed to play when they stopped. My mind went a complete blank. I knew I had forgotten my first entry. I thought, gosh, what'll I do? Then it went through my mind that I could just faint. So I just fainted.' The image of him slumping deceitfully to the floor was indelibly printed on my mind. More than once while sitting in the soloist's spot myself I've had to swat the image away.

Then there is the troubling thought that you have not prepared well enough, that you are going to disappoint everyone. This is very annoying if you know perfectly well you've done all you can beforehand. If you are playing an unfamiliar instrument, as pianists almost always are, you may sit there worrying that you won't be able to control the keys when you play your opening phrases. You imagine that the members of the orchestra sitting around you are probably thinking that you didn't deserve this chance. The conductor seems to be ignoring you, probably because he despises you. And aren't those people in the front row sneering? Surely your clothes were not this tight when you tried them on at home? 'I can't do this' is your overriding thought.

Simultaneously, you realise that these thoughts are supremely unhelpful and that you have only minutes to stop them if they are not to ruin the performance. It is masochistic to picture yourself as a foetal mouse when the truth is that you were specifically chosen to be tonight's soloist. You were asked months or years before and have been preparing for this concert for a long time. Many people in the audience will have bought their tickets because of this very piece, for it is well known that all the world loves a soloist. Some of them will eagerly be trying to guess what exciting outfit you will wear, and some look forward to the spectacle of musical combat between a lone gladiator and a baying orchestral crowd. It should, indeed, be a moment to feel king-sized.

And actually, everything would be a lot more pleasant if one felt that way. There probably are soloists who are not troubled by doubts, who feel terrific as they stand there listening to the orchestral opening, lapping up the audience's attention. Perhaps they positively look forward to dazzling us the moment they get the chance. They paw the ground impatiently as the music creeps towards their first entry. Certainly there are some seasoned racehorses on the concerto circuit who do this night after night, and no doubt feel absolutely confident that the audience has done the right thing by giving up an evening at the fireside in order to come and hear them. But this kind of soloist probably comes from a rather different culture, and in any case I, as an observer, don't find such nervelessness interesting. I don't want them only to fight the orchestra and win; I want them to fight themselves and win.

I have a friend who has run some workshops on performance nerves. She advocates just listening to the orchestra and trying to forget yourself. Sinking your ego into the whole musical event could be a great idea, but I have tried this, and found that there comes a moment when I have to retrieve my individual self from the collective whole and accept that the soloist's role is mine alone. We are not, in fact, all going to do this together. Going into denial about the soloist's role runs counter to everything the concerto means in dramatic terms. It is *about* the emergence of the one from the mass. So there is no point in my sitting there pretending that I'm watching someone else do this on television. To be this splendid One, I need my mind, so there is no point in quietening it, but I have to learn how to let negative thoughts wither in the bud. I must not waste my time thinking the wrong thoughts! I must let myself think the right thoughts (whatever they are)! And usually it is just at this point in my reflections that the orchestra throws down the gauntlet, and it is my moment to shine.

V is for Very

One of our frequent rehearsal topics is how much larger than life things have to be on stage to come across as life-sized to the audience. A famous violinist once said that things had to be 120 per cent at home in order to be ninety per cent on the platform. He was referring to the player's degree of preparedness, but his remark might apply to other aspects of performing as well. As players, we accept that in a big hall there are certain levels of volume and certain types of gesture that will not be received by listeners with the same effect they have on us, sitting close together. What seems perfectly clear in the rehearsal room may seem underdone on the stage.

In practice we find that for concerts, things have sometimes to be 'scaled up' in order to counteract the minimising effects of distance. We know there's a danger that we will look small and sound small too. We find ourselves using the dreaded word 'projection', now a vital part of the technical armoury of all students who intend to have concert careers. In rehearsal we use it to describe our attempts to send the sound rippling out to the back of the hall. When rehearsing concertos – for example the Beethoven Triple – we always speak about the sheer volume needed to cut through an orchestra of eighty people all playing instruments set up for modern symphony halls. Niceties of phrasing and dialogue become rather subsidiary to the effort of making a big enough sound. Our violinist threatened to come to rehearsals wearing a T-shirt he had been given in California, bearing the slogan 'Play f—ing loud'.

Yet there is always a contrary view. While recognising that things have to be writ large in order to seem big enough, we also think that audiences can tell when something is being unnaturally scaled up. Though sitting far away, people don't lose their sense of body language. Even if someone looks small on the stage, people know when a performer is over-acting, or making unusually big movements for their benefit. They can hear when the instrumental tone is strained through over-exertion. Clearly there's a fine line between being big, and trying too hard to be big. We often hope that instead of wilfully broadcasting our sound to the back rows, we can do the opposite: draw the audience in. This means developing a concentration and intensity which will make the audience want to focus on us. It will be their turn to minimise the distance between us, by reaching out mentally across the space. And actually, this often works, even in the largest halls. We believe that if we produce the right quality of sound, listeners can imagine themselves close to us on stage, hearing things as we hear them, with appropriate intensity but no exaggeration.

This 'no exaggeration' is a conundrum we gnaw at all the time. Is it even possible to be a performer and not exaggerate? We know that leaping the bounds of the everyday, painting things in bright colours, is an inescapable ingredient of the art of performance. Yet as I write the word 'inescapable' I realise that it is a revealing choice of word. Would I like to escape it? Yes, I would. I would often like to escape the task of 'selling' the music to the audience. I would like to present the music as vividly as it presents itself to me, not more. Yet since I first started having music lessons, it was put to me that this was not enough. Using an intimate manner, for example, has always been suspect. Playing things as quietly as you would play them in your own living room was simply not adequate on stage. One had to learn a new register of expressions: a kind of platform 'quiet', a platform 'loud'. One had to discover that fast music might sound even faster in a big room; conversely, that slow music needed to expand in a big hall in order to have the same grand effect that it has in your home. The scores I prepared for concert performance were littered with instructions from teachers: 'More!' 'Project!' 'Bigger!' They battled against what they saw as my propensity for understatement. I thought I was telling it like it was, but they thought nobody would be able to hear me. It seemed that my own private view of music needed to undergo a process of glorification before it was suitable for the stage.

Composers usually write a few words of instruction at the beginning of pieces, and the words refer to tempo and expression. The word 'very' appears often. Very fast, very slow, very strong, very singing, very expressive. Very lively, very strict, very quiet. Intensification is the name of the game. One notices that in earlier music the simple instruction 'lively', 'flowing' or 'fast' was enough. In the Romantic and modern eras, these basic words seem to be more and more qualified with words meaning 'very'. As fast as possible, as loud as possible. The Italian signs for soft and loud, 'p' for piano and 'f' for forte, are more and more seen in their multiplied versions, *pp* and *ff* or even *ppp* and *fff*, meaning very, very soft or loud. 'Molto' appears all over the place as an augmentation. *Molto allegro*, *Molto espressivo*, *Molto cantabile*. The Italian superlative '–issimo' is often encountered in such words as *Prestissimo* (extremely fast), or *Vivacissimo* (extremely lively). Was 'fast' not enough, was 'lively' not enough? Do we not know how to 'sing' without being told to be 'very singing'? Is being expressive not as good as being awfully expressive? Did composers feel that those simple words wouldn't come to life without an intensifier?

Whether this trend towards exaggeration is linked historically with the growing size of concert halls, the increased dynamic range of instruments, or whether it is an index of the growing importance of personal expression, I could not say. But through the nineteenth century there is a trend away from simple descriptions of tempo to more and more extreme instructions. In Schumann's music, for example, his advice is often heated: 'very excited', 'extremely inward', 'faster and faster', and the highly characteristic 'Aüsserst bewegt' (exceedingly agitated). Sometimes he seems to repent of this style: 'but not too much' starts to creep in, and sometimes there is no tempo indication except for the mild remark, 'not too fast'. Yet even in these counter-instructions the concept of 'too' is present. We musicians are all in the business of making things 'very' this or that, or not *too* much this or that. The whole dish is flavoured with exaggeration.

If I think about it, I suppose that I have been trying to see how much I can pull back from the arena of exaggeration and rediscover the original scale of the music as it first struck me. I'm not talking about how it struck me when I heard someone else perform it, because those memories are flavoured with someone else's platform manner, but how it struck me when I learned the music myself. There's a line in my imagination that separates how I feel the music from how I think I have to present it to listeners, and I always seem to be crossing and re-crossing that line. Sometimes I cross it and the music crosses it with me; other times I cross the line and the music stays on the other side. It may seem that certain music needs a bit of aggrandisement to work properly in concert. More often it seems that certain music has become distorted through years of careless platform overkill. Grand gestures have become part of the accepted way of performing certain pieces, even though the composers have indicated nothing of the kind. Successive generations of performers have preserved the gestures and timing of older performers (often known to us through recordings), though the original meaning of those gestures may have become either inscrutable or fossilised.

At the same time you cannot forget that the piano in your home has the same range as the instrument you play in the concert hall. We never use amplification, so we have to address the purely practical necessity of being heard, and in a big hall that usually just means playing louder. The only place it is not necessary to play louder is in the recording studio, but that is a whole different story. Experience shows that even if one thinks one can play at a domestic volume in a recording session, the listener will bring a certain expectation of what music generally sounds like in the concert hall, and even the musicians cannot forget their usual efforts to intensify the music. Removing our habitual sound projection can suddenly make us feel dull and small, especially when we have prepared for the recording with a series of concert performances, and have incorporated the audiences' responses into our playing. So making records certainly does not provide the simple opportunity to 'be oneself' and play naturally in front of the microphones.

It remains a dream of mine to escape the world of 'very', the constant need to scale everything up from the proportions it has in my mind's eye. Sadly, this is not an easy time in which to realise the dream. People have got so used to loud music, to huge stage effects, to shouting and posturing and guitar-bashing. Teenagers regard loud music as part of their identity. Cars roll down the street with windows open and music blaring so loud that I can hear it inside the house. We constantly hear that when our fifteen minutes of fame are upon us, we have to seize the moment to be as colourful, as startling, as possible. It is in this climate that the 'Play f--ing loud' T-shirt slogan is not a joke, but a sober piece of advice. I might prefer to wear a sweatshirt reading, 'Play quietly and make people listen', but I'd have to get one made specially. Meanwhile, I find myself turning with pleasure to the instructions of Mozart, for whom 'Allegro' and 'Andante' and 'Vivace' were enough. And so they should be, for they have sufficient meanings. We need more verification, not more 'very'-fication.

W is for Weighing up Praise and Criticism

In the world of classical music it's usual for advanced students and young professionals to continue having lessons, attending masterclasses, and seeking advice from players they admire. This means that well into their twenties they are submitting their playing for criticism, often in public, at a time when most young people would expect to have finished their training. Obviously it takes a special kind of open-mindedness to keep on asking whether your playing could still be improved. On the other hand, these mature students are old enough to be able to take or leave the teachers' advice.

Recently I coached a young Japanese chamber group. They were all excellent players, but what struck me most about them was their insecurity. Their stage manner wasn't as convincing as it could have been, given their finesse; they radiated a sense of 'Please do not find us good if you do not think it appropriate.' Therefore, as well as giving musical advice, I decided that my main task was to bolster their egos. I told them that they were fine players, but that they were wasting energy in self-doubt when it would be much more productive to use that energy in communicating with their listeners. They seemed to find this useful.

A couple of months later I had a letter from them. They had just returned from what the French would call a 'stage de perfectionnement', a high-level music seminar with Middle European professors. They reported that after they had played for the first time, the teacher had folded his arms in an ominous silence before saying, 'Well, well, well. Where to begin? . . . Let me ask you what *you* thought was wrong with your performance.' They were taken aback, but one recovered enough to say, 'It was perhaps not so unanimous now as it is in our rehearsals.' 'No,' said the professor. 'That's not it. Any other ideas?' Another player said, 'Perhaps we do not understand Beethoven's style?' 'I didn't mean that.' Someone else said, 'I think maybe we did not make the structure clear.' There was a silence. Then the teacher said, 'Well, if you do not know, I will tell you. It was not in tune.'

Now to an observer it seemed clear that such a professorial gambit should be taken with a pinch of salt. It was the equivalent of seeing someone in a glorious outfit and only commenting that their shoes were not polished. Or like looking at a beautiful garden and only saying that there were places that hadn't been weeded. To me it was obvious that the focus of this lesson had been trivial, perhaps deliberately so. However, what I hadn't expected was the students' reaction. They felt their faults must have been so basic that there was no point in speaking of higher matters. After several such lessons, they were so dejected that they could hardly play in front of the audience. But maddeningly, they seemed to think that this would turn out to be a salutary experience, a kicking they probably deserved if they were only smart enough to figure out why. Moreover, they thought that because I (a woman) had been nice and this other teacher (a man) had been horrible, *he was the one who must be right*. My praise was a candle easily blown out by his criticism.

I wrote back, 'I must advise you not to be depressed by lack of compliments. If a teacher is critical, it doesn't necessarily mean that they are "more right" than another who appreciates your playing. Sometimes, not paying compliments is a way to have power.' It was my turn to feel despondent.

When I was a postgraduate student I spent a very happy semester at the Banff Arts Centre in Canada with my former group Domus. Instead of having a permanent teaching staff, the Banff Centre had a rota of visiting players and professors who stayed for periods ranging from just a few days to a week or two. Students were invited to sign up for lessons with any or all of these, though we were warned that if we were unsure of our own style and ideas, it would be unsettling to have lessons from too many people. We had already had several years of concert experience together, and we felt pretty sure of our aims, so we signed up for lessons with absolutely everybody.

It was both fascinating and enriching, and I wouldn't have missed it for the world, but what became clear was that each visiting professor looked at things from his or her own angle and 'with their own agenda', as we didn't say in those days. We took the same piece of chamber music – Fauré's C minor piano quartet – to umpteen different gurus and let them shine their own particular lights on it. Gradually we realised that we had been told our playing was delightfully French, not French enough, too 'Germanic', too piano-oriented, too string-oriented, too democratic, and not democratic enough. One person applauded our

British reserve, while another felt it was handicapping us. We were told that we were pleasingly individual, and also that we were not unanimous enough. Someone told us he had never heard the work so faithfully and idiomatically played, while another felt we needed to stop looking at the score and let our imaginations run riot. Memorably, I was told by the distinguished cellist János Starker to 'stop playing the piece as a blonde and try to play like a redhead', an instruction that is still beyond me.

It became obvious that there was no overarching advice that took everything into account and transcended the personal. Furthermore, within our group, people varied quite a bit in their assessment of which advice was true or 'right for us'. We didn't even agree amongst ourselves about who had most truly held a mirror up to us. According to our different temperaments, some felt that praise was inspiring and helpful, while others felt that only criticism should be taken seriously. Finally we realised that, at the end of the day, all we could do was to understand the piece as well as we could, given our own characters and contexts. Even good advice was sometimes impossible to follow because of who we were. This was chastening, but also uplifting. We had to find something that rang true *to us*.

But knowing what rings true to you is no easy matter. How, after all, are our personal beliefs formed? Many young performers are happy to take on trust the views of respected or beloved teachers. It may take years to develop one's own individual viewpoint, and in fact it may not be possible, or even desirable, to be original. Advanced students are often in thrall to the opinions their teachers have of them, especially if they have only one teacher. If their teacher sees them in a negative way, it takes the strongest of characters to feel confident nonetheless. Sadly, the converse is not true. If a teacher gives lots of praise and support, a self-critical student may feel that the teacher's powers of discernment must be lacking. For a teacher, deciding whether to praise or blame becomes fraught with peril. Some students open up like flowers when you support them, while others need that piece of grit in the oyster shell which encourages them to make a pearl.

X is for the Unknown

For the crossword enthusiast, the appearance of the word 'unknown' in a clue usually signals that the answer will contain the letters 'x' or 'y', mathematical symbols for unknown numbers. X has always seemed to me more appropriate as a designation of the unknown, a symbol barring the way to the territory of the known.

When people speak about musicians who play from written notes, and in particular classical musicians, they often compare them with improvising musicians, and say that playing from a score is much less creative because 'everything is known'. Yet all performers learn the hard way that a musical score is not a complete blueprint for a performance of the piece. The score is a set of instructions for the musicians, but because notation is such an inexact science, many things remain unknown, and always will. What we have on the printed page is little more than a code giving the approximate pitches and rhythms of the music, with a few words signalling mood and speed. Benjamin Britten once remarked that he sometimes felt quite daunted when he opened the score of Schubert's song cycle *Winterreise*, because 'there seems to be nothing on the page'. Here is a good example of a great piece of music whose score barely hints at the atmosphere and profundity that its performance can generate.

The score cannot perform itself, nor transform itself into sound. Only a real musician can do that, and he or she has to supply ingredients not specified anywhere, perhaps not even envisaged in detail by the composer, who might not have had a very clear idea of what would work in performance. Every musician who picks up the score will realise it in a different way, not only because of differences of musical and intellectual approach, but also because of their own instrumental technique and personal sound, and because of myriad unknown factors to do with their society and the time they live in. If there is more than one musician involved, the ingredients are multiplied.

A little while ago I tried to find out something on the Internet about a piece of eighteenth-century Spanish keyboard music. I was invited to 'click here to hear a performance of the piece'. But it was not a performance. It was a computer-generated rendition of the notes and rhythms without the least dynamic variety or expression. Indeed, though it reproduced the notes in the score, there was so much missing that I hardly recognised it as the piece I had been learning. The known was there, but it seemed pathetically inadequate. What was missing was the unknown, which clearly the composer had neglected to notate, and which a computer had no chance of guessing. And it was these missing unknowns – the mood, the momentum, the overall shape, the variation of tone and timing, the spirit – that prevented the synthesised version not only from being a performance, but even from being an artistic entity. Reduced to a sequence of notes *alone*, the musical impulse behind the piece was annihilated. It seemed clear that the notes were the tip of the iceberg. The unknown, or the nonspecified, ingredients were the larger part of the work, or to be more precise, of its effect in performance.

Even if a musician plays a single note, he or she cannot know whether the composer ever imagined it like that. For a start, there are stylistic questions. Let's say the player uses vibrato. Is that what the composer expected? Let's say they play on a violin with metal strings. Would that have been a surprise? Has standard pitch changed since the composer's day – is it higher now, and does that make things sound different? What if the player trained in France, or America, or Japan? Would their way of producing sound come as a surprise – their attack, their volume? Suppose the player is responding to the written instruction 'fast'. What did someone of two hundred years ago mean by 'fast', what vision would they have had in their mind's eye: a running man, a galloping horse? Now that things move faster, has our concept of 'fast' changed? Do we now imagine a computer thinking, a jet plane flying? What about an instruction like 'lively'? As lively as a happy dog in the eighteenth century, as lively as a clubber taking Ecstasy pills in the twentieth? These things are unknown for both sides. Just as the player cannot know what the composer expected, the composer cannot know how the player will interpret his signs. Composer and interpreter try to catch one another's eye through the veiled network of the musical score.

When you listen to a performance of improvised music, its course is unknown, though the significance of this is often exaggerated. Many types of improvised music around the world, for example, follow rules almost as strict as classical composers do when writing in tried and tested forms. Folk, ritual and community music usually use a well-defined vocabulary of melodies, accompaniments and gestures. There are only a few kinds of music, such as free jazz, that consciously spurn traditional forms and set out to do without any of what they perceive as lazy props and reminders. However, the result is by no means automatically satisfying. Sometimes inspiration strikes and a wonderful story is told by the players. Sometimes the players interact in an engrossing way. But often there is a meandering, haphazard quality to the music which fails to engage the audience. As a listener one sometimes senses that not only are the notes unknown, but the emotions and the shapes too. Often the music emerges as a stream of consciousness, with all the inconsequentiality that any few minutes of a stream of consciousness may have. Fans of this type of music are fond of talking about 'the journey' that a piece of improvised music undertakes. But not every step on to a road is the beginning of a journey. If the participants remain outside their own front door, or wander down the road and forget where they were meant to be going, it is not a journey at all.

It might seem that there are more unknowns in non-notated music than in notated music, but I am not sure that this is the case. In composed music the notes are known, and this also means that people get to hear other performances of them. Other people's interpretations, and what listeners say about them, build up a rich texture of hopes and fears around works that have proved moving and uplifting in performance. Great music often exploits the layers of different emotions and moods that can co-exist in the human soul. Such layering is planned and intended by the composer (think of the bittersweet quartets and sextets in operas) and performers work long and hard to bring out all the meanings. They are aware of the love that audiences already feel for these pieces, and of the emotional catharsis that hearing and seeing a great performance can deliver. But emotional catharsis is not a simple matter to achieve, and nobody can achieve it without working on themselves as well as working at the score. Anyone who has enjoyed a great performance of something will often feel a sense of mystery for long afterwards. What was actually done, how was it done, and who did it?

This kind of complexity is very rarely encountered in improvised music, though one must admit straight away that there is a lot of printed music that is likewise meandering and trivial. It is not in the nature of something made up on the spur of the moment that it encompasses all sorts of poignantly timed collisions of mood and idea. Such moments can, of course, occur in improvised music by chance, but the artistic effect is often lost because what comes before and what comes after are unsatisfyingly random. There have been improvising geniuses like Charlie Parker or John Coltrane who operated at a high level of consciousness and across long spans of musical time, but they are the exception. A lot of respect is given to people who start out 'on a voyage of discovery', but notes tumbling out as they occur to the improviser are not necessarily imaginative, as I know from my own experience of playing jazz. The effect of improvised music is often linear, a thread unspooling in time. This may seems perfectly appropriate to the casual context of the performance. But it often seems to mean that heights and depths are not reached, perhaps not even attempted.

With both written and made-up music, one could say that

the sky is the limit. And with both types of music one could also say that the result gets nowhere near the sky. But whatever people think about the 'creative' potential of improvised music, there is no guarantee that it will outreach notated music in its effect, nor that it will actually be more creative. However serious improvised music is, and however enjoyable it is to listen to, it is often limited in what it sets out to do, and limited in what it does. In that sense its parameters are known, even if its notes are not. But this is a different kind of art from that which sets out, using a composed work, to do justice to something deep and strange. The musicians who immerse themselves in this kind of task are grappling with at least as many unknowns as the champions of improvised music. Certain pieces of music have been known for a long time to be rich enough in meanings and effects to change people's lives. Nobody could make them up on the spur of the moment, not even the composer (with the possible exception of Mozart, who was said to conceive of pieces in a single moment). They need work and planning, thought, experience, understanding and dedication. But no composer has discovered how to notate the sometimes paradoxical ingredients needed to make a performance come alive and the music speak powerfully across the years. Indeed, no one could know in advance what might be needed from any given set of performers. The known, enduring qualities of great music need enormous quantities of unknown, unknowable ingredients to make them whole.

Y is for Youngsters

How many other professions claim their practitioners from childhood right through to advanced old age? Teaching, politics, science, industry, banking, Civil Service, medicine, office work, architecture, design, the law – all these begin in earnest when people are mature. Hardly any of my non-musician friends could sit down and write an essay about the youngsters in their profession, because there aren't any. 'Young lawyers I have known'. 'Gifted investment bankers under the age of ten'. Sounds ridiculous, doesn't it? But music calls to people of all ages. Why? Perhaps because it can be enjoyed at so many levels: aural, instinctive, emotional, nervous, physical. A mature person can add intellectual skills, but even a child can get a lot out of, and put a lot into, music.

Now, when I look around my musician friends and see how many of them are struggling with 'burn-out', I reflect that in most cases they have been hard at it since they were little children. No wonder they long for a break after practising every day for thirty-five or forty years! We 'athletes of the small muscles' are obsessed with keeping supple. At a time when most people have been engaged in their professions for only a decade, many musicians have been tackling those daily scales and arpeggios for a quarter of a century. More to the point, if musicians have been good at it since childhood – as all my colleagues were – they will have been putting their bodies through the strain of concert performance for a very long time.

When I was little and started taking part in concerts and competitions, my parents discovered that playing a concert was not just like any other task I had been set. To get to the point of being able to perform in public, and from memory, I had to psych myself up to quite a pitch. This involved not sleeping properly for days or weeks beforehand, not finding it easy to concentrate on other things, and sometimes suffering nervous physical disorders such as skin problems and dizzy spells. After the performance, I was too keyed up to sleep. My mother hit on the remedy of putting on a record of dance music and encouraging me to jump around until I got tired. This worked fine when I was little, but of course no teenager would consent to jump around in the family living room, so there followed years of trying to unwind by stomping about moodily and reading late into the night. Even though I liked those concerts, the strain of performance seemed to necessitate a huge winding-up and a winding-down afterwards, none of it very compatible with everyday life. In all this I don't think I was unusual; any parent of a musically precocious child will probably recognise the description. Even today, people who spend time with me on concert days get to know the routine of preoccupation and withdrawal that seems to be an inescapable part of them, for me and for most of my colleagues.

Once when I was about ten years old, my piano teacher organised a concert in which a few of her best pupils played concertos with an orchestra. I was the youngest performer. This was a really big deal, which even inspired my mother to get out her sewing machine and make me 'a red dress with a sticky-out skirt'. I played Mozart's Piano Concerto in A major K488, though goodness knows how – as mentioned in the essay on Difficulty, when I re-learned it last year for a concert, I found it very challenging. Anyway, at ten years old I enjoyed the performance and don't remember any difficulty in playing from memory. Afterwards, one of the university's professors of music, the composer Hans Gál, said to my teacher that 'only the very young or the very old can play like that'. At the time I didn't know what he meant. Was he saying that it was very shaky and feeble? Did he mean that I sounded as though I was moments away from not being able to play the piano at all? But no, from the beaming smiles on the faces of the adults I realised that it was a compliment. Only the very young or the very old? So did children have some quality that they lost when they became adults, but got back when they were ancient? At the age of ten I couldn't imagine what that might be. All my lessons had been directed forwards, looking towards the time when I would be advanced enough to do this or that, experienced enough to know my way, good enough to be compared with grown-ups, to be a grown-up musician myself. I had always taken it for granted that grown-up pianists were better than child pianists. Weren't they?

Afterwards, my teacher explained that Gál had meant there was a simplicity in the way I played which could only be captured in childhood, and then maybe again years later, when a person was wise enough to have lost their vanity and self-importance. Naturally, I was unimpressed by the idea that I had played simply. I wanted to seem tremendously sophisticated, mature beyond my years. But I accepted that there were people who found something charming in my childish ways, and that because I was the youngest they were especially pleased by me. And now, of course, as an adult I relish the playing of unspoiled children (I use the adjective carefully). But I was also left with the notion – largely correct as it turned out – that the whole era of grown-up playing, in between childhood and old age, was far from simple. Its complications turned out to be essential ingredients of great performances, but that is another story.

The two Hungarian teachers of whom I often speak, Sándor Végh and György Sebök, both talked about themselves as heedless young performers. Végh compared his own case with that of Yehudi Menuhin, who as the world knows was one of the most naturally talented young violinists ever heard. Végh said that both he and Menuhin had reached a point in young adulthood where they started to think about what they were doing and how they were doing it. 'I was lucky,' said Sándor Végh. 'I thought about what I was doing, and I started to understand how. Then I dropped my understanding inside' (he said, indicating his stomach). '*I digested my talent*. Poor Menuhin was not so lucky. He started to wonder *how* he was doing what he was doing. Suddenly he was afraid. When he started to wonder how he was doing it, it did not work any more.' To say that it did not work was, of course, a gross exaggeration, but we had recently had the opportunity to see Menuhin in concert and we all knew what he meant. In fact, Menuhin impressed us deeply as a musician, but it was chastening to see his shaking bow-arm and his frowns of concentration and distress. It seemed clear that something – critical thought, I suppose – had intervened between his early effortlessness and his adult style. Yet Menuhin's early style was not characterised by 'simplicity'. It was a preternaturally rounded, mature approach which, one might have guessed, had already passed through the fire of self-scrutiny and come out the other side.

György Sebök also described the unshakeable confidence he had as a young pianist. As a teenager he was famous for his sightreading abilities, and even had the nerve to sightread in concerts. Eventually he was offered the chance of a regular 'live' spot on Budapest's radio station. He dared himself to take volumes of piano music into the studio, wait until the red light went on to indicate that the live broadcast was in progress, and then open one of the volumes at random and play whatever he saw in front of him. We didn't get to hear any tapes of the results, but he assured us they were good. In his case it was not a dawning self-consciousness that destroyed his sense of ease, but the Second World War. Gradually realising how precarious everything was, seeing people's lives torn up at a moment's notice, witnessing the suffering – all this profoundly impressed on him that there was no security. He lost his childish sense that everything was going to be all right. He remained a good sightreader, but lost the wish to flaunt his invulnerability. 'It was like being chased from Paradise,' he said.

Chased from Paradise. It seemed clear from these comments that there is a tricky phase to be negotiated between being a young musician and a mature one, and *digesting your talent* is the clue to doing it. Many youngsters who excel at music get a lot of praise, support and status from their families, schools, music teachers. When they step out into the wider world, most people lose that status.

Negotiating the passage from talented child to successful adult musician often seems to boil down to realising that you are doing it because *you* want to do it, not because other people want you to do it. This may sound simple, but has caused many musicians to stumble. Non-musicians don't face this task, because most people don't carry on one activity intensely from childhood into adulthood like musicians do. There are musicians whose progression from youngster to grown-up is more or less a straight line. They progress through music courses and summer schools and youth orchestras, patiently acquiring technique and knowledge of repertoire, arriving at music college with every appetite for a full-time course of study. Their journey from young musician to adult musician has a fortunate gradient, not peaking too soon. But all those people I know who were exceptionally able as youngsters, or more particularly were put under the spotlight by ambitious adults, have wrestled with the question, 'Is it really me who wants this?'

When I was little I thought that older people were bound to be better than me, and the more experienced, the better. It would never have occurred to me that given the choice between the young me and an artist of international distinction, concert promoters would choose me (and they didn't). But the luckiest and most confident of today's youngsters have a very different experience. Young musicians are now the flavour of the year. So many competitions have come into existence, almost all of them for youngsters. Prizes and concert opportunities are showered on them, and our present cult of celebrity and physical beauty has dovetailed effectively with the public's perennial interest in gifted youngsters. Economic factors play a part in their increasing success. A gifted but inexperienced young artist, eager to notch up concert performances, and perhaps backed by an Arts Trust or a corporate sponsor, will agree to play a concert for much less than an older, more seasoned artist would charge. For many concert promoters it is an irresistible combination. Not only do they get a fresh, attractive young artist, but they get them cheaply! One would like to think that promoters stop to wonder which artist will provide the more satisfying experience, but I am not sure that they do.

When I was first making my way in the profession, finding it tough, I sometimes asked the help of people further along the professional road than I was. I asked them to put my name forward if they heard of concert opportunities. They always said, 'You have to be patient. Your turn will come! Concerts go to experienced players who have worked hard and have spent a long time getting to that point. It's only right that they should be given the work. They have paid their dues. You will get there eventually.' Years passed, and I paid my own dues. But by then the tide had turned, and experienced artists were no longer the summit of promoters' ambition. They were starting to say, 'Sorry we can't have you this year – we've been given the chance to book young artists from the such-and-such scheme, or winners of the such-and-such competition. It's cheaper for us, and our audiences like to see young folk just starting out.' Somewhere along the line I seemed to have missed my age-group's turn to be the flavour of the month.

For the best of today's young artists the musical world is their oyster. But they, in turn, may find that the bulk of their concert opportunities came when they were young, and they may wonder how to sustain a career in mid-life.

Perhaps the audience's taste will switch back to mature artists, and today's youngsters will be a fortunate generation – in favour both when they are young and when they are experienced. Luckily, music doesn't only start early in a person's life; it goes on exceptionally late as well. There are still fine musicians playing concerts in their seventies, eighties and even nineties (as the pianist Horszowski demonstrated). If I am still playing at that point, maybe I will have the satisfaction of hearing that only the very young or the very old can play like that.

Z is for Zen

Watching something being done well has always interested me. It doesn't matter whether it is something I know about, or something I know almost nothing about, like sport. Anyone who has reached a high level of achievement, in whatever field, is interesting to watch. People who are good at things are good at them in all kinds of different ways, of course. Some wrestle with themselves and go through contortions. Some concentrate and frown. Some make things look easy. As I watch them I'm always looking for an extra factor, very difficult to put into words, which interests me particularly. It's something to do with a level of supreme technical skill allied to a relaxed mind. When these qualities are combined, one often sees a coalescing of actor and action which demonstrates a different level of consciousness, one beyond the everyday.

There is a difference between people who are merely skilful and people who have gone a stage further, producing a result which is sometimes described as 'natural' and sometimes as 'miraculous', though in fact it can be both. You know it when you see it, but what is it? It often seems to be linked to high technical skill, but the technique itself is not the decisive factor. Rather it is that in the long struggle to acquire great technique, people have to master themselves. They learn to put themselves at the service of whatever it is they are trying to do, ultimately focusing on the thing itself instead of the means of achieving it. The superb balance, the finely honed physique, the trained muscles all become subsidiary to a special kind of joyful awareness in which everything seems to be easy, or in which it seems obvious what to do. They don't even have to think about it, they just do it. Actually, it's misleading to say that they 'don't even have to think'. Thought is somehow irrelevant.

Since teenage years I have been a fan of the little classic, *Zen in the Art of Archery* by Eugen Herrigel, a German philosopher who wished to study the oriental philosophy of Zen and was advised to do so through the study of archery, a skill he had never tried. Appreciating that there was a long tradition of studying Zen 'in action' through all kinds of practical and martial arts, he accepted the challenge of archery. His book describes the long process during which he learned the several techniques necessary to make a shot. For months he learned how to draw the bow without ever releasing the arrow. For further months he learned how to hold the bow taut with his shoulders relaxed. He then moved on to learning how to release the bowstring without flinching. Only after a year or so was he allowed to shoot at a target, and by then his perception of it had changed, as his teacher intended.

It became clear to him that the months of learning to draw the bow, hold it taut and so on were not, ultimately, 'about' the bow. They were, rather, about him. Through the perfecting of isolated parts of his technique, he learned to focus entirely on his state of mind, and to reach realms of awareness he had not reached before. His teacher wished to empty him of ego and self-consciousness. The student had to learn to give up completely the desire to hit the target, a step so delayed in his lessons that it came to seem irrelevant. He describes vividly how, after a year of intense training, he felt the arrow leave the bow without any conscious calculation on his part. This was not, he stresses, a matter of accidentally 'letting go'. The crucial point was that in the mastering of his own state of consciousness, he had ceased to think of himself as the one doing the shooting, and the target as the one being shot. He and the target were no longer two opposing objects. To say that the archer and the target had become one reality may seem utterly fanciful, but when he experienced this for the first time, aware that the arrow was flying effortlessly to its destination (as if it had never been separate from it), his teacher bowed low to him and remarked, 'There! *It* shot.'

The idea that 'it' shot, rather than 'he shot', may seem stupid or far-fetched to a Western reader. But anyone who has experienced this 'artless art' will know that it is difficult to word it any other way. The 'it' that shot was not him, but nor was it not him. Perhaps there is no way to write about such an experience, because in the words of the Zen scholar D. T. Suzuki, 'Words are liable to detach themselves from realities and turn into conceptions.' However, there are people in many fields who have shared Herrigel's experience of this mysterious unification of the doer and the thing done. They might not call it Zen. Indeed, they might not call it anything at all, because it is a hard thing to name. But it is an experience available to anyone who has learned a high degree of relaxed focus. It is not available to people who think that they can get it by being lazy, by not trying, by not thinking, by letting the unconscious rampage away, or by leaving things to the mercies of chance. In the words of D. T. Suzuki, 'The archer ceases to be conscious of himself as the one who is engaged in hitting the bulls-eye which confronts him. This state of unconsciousness is realised only when, completely empty and rid of the self, he becomes one with the perfecting of his technical skill, though there is in it something of a quite different order which cannot be attained by any progressive study of the art.'*

How is this relevant to the study of music and its performance? Well, any good performer after intense study and preparation may experience moments, even long tracts, of Zen-like concentration. It doesn't feel as if one is playing oneself, but as if 'it' is playing. A player may have this experience when alone or on a concert platform; it doesn't seem to be dependent on adrenalin, though some performers feel that the heightened sense of occasion makes it more likely. Nor is it a matter of losing concentration. We have all seen performers who seem to be going through the motions mechanically, on automatic pilot. That is not at all what I mean by saying that 'it' is playing. The 'it', really, is something for which none of us has a better word. 'It' is not an outside agency, like God or a guardian angel. One might say that the player and the music do not remain separate, just as the archer and the target do not. There ceases to be one who is doing the playing, and a separate piece of music that is played.

Taking the image of the space between the archer and the target, one could liken it to the intellectual space between the person doing the work, and the work itself. This space

* Daisetz T. Suzuki, *Zen and Japanese Culture* (Princeton University Press, 1959)

is usually filled with thoughts, desires and fears belonging to the player. Indeed, travelling across that space is the stuff of practice and rehearsal. But it is possible to experience the collapse of the intellectual space separating musician from music, and with it the collapse of the unhelpful thoughts and fears that live there. Just as the Zen archer may feel that there is no distance between himself and his target, the musician may feel that there is no distinction between him- or herself and the music.

I am not speaking about the over-identification that causes some players wildly to demonstrate their attachment to the music. I'm also not speaking about emotional identification with the music, because this is nothing to do with emotions. It is, ultimately, something simple, but the simplicity is not to be confused with an elementary approach, or with deliberate regression to being childish (both of which are commonly seen). D. T. Suzuki says that it cannot be attained by any progressive study, but it seems that it cannot be attained without progressive study either. Equipped with a fine technique, players can reach a mobile state of being in which they are able to respond to anything. Nothing comes as a surprise, not even inspiration. In this state, their actions arise naturally out of the unconscious, and the notes fly out by themselves.

Such a state is difficult for today's musicians to achieve, because our audiences have a taste for displays of ego, and if you are under pressure to strut and fret your hour upon the stage, it is almost impossible to empty yourself. Nevertheless, the concert platform is a good place to work towards this experience, because generally speaking you don't get to be on a concert platform unless you have reached a high degree of skill and commitment. In my experience it is precisely in those concerts for which one is super-prepared that the little glimpses of Zen are most likely to happen. The feeling that it was not 'I' who played, but 'it', is no easier to put into words at the end of this essay than it was at the beginning. But even tiny doses are enough to keep one searching for the opportunity to repeat the experience. 'It' can be found in every aspect of life, I know, but music is a very good field in which to harvest it.